Who Will Save
Our Children?

Who Will Save
Our Children?

The Plight of the Jamaican Child in the 1990s

Claudette Crawford-Brown

Canoe Press University of the West Indies
1A Aqueduct Flats Mona
Kingston 7 Jamaica

03   02   01   00   99   5   4   3   2   1

CATALOGUING IN PUBLICATION DATA

Crawford-Brown, Claudette.
Who will save our children? The plight of the
Jamaican child in the nineties / Claudette
Crawford-Brown.
p.cm.
Includes bibliographical references.
ISBN: 976-8125-30-6

1. Children — Jamaica. 2. Child welfare — Jamaica.
3. Child abuse — Jamaica. 4. Parenting — Jamaica.
I. Title.

HQ792.J3C73 1999   362.7 dc-20

Dedicated to Vie and Ben Hawthorne
Thank you for believing in me

"THIS WORLD"
(One view of the world written by an eleven-year-old Jamaican child)

If You Listen To This World
What Do You Think You'd Hear?
I Think You'd Hear It Crying Out In Anguish, Sorrow And Fear,
You Wouldn't Even Notice The Joy And Laughter Here,
You Would Hear It Crying Out In Anguish, Sorrow And Fear.

If You Looked Into This World,
What Do You Think You'd See?
You'd See the Poverty Staring in Your Faces,
You Wouldn't See the Joy, Warmth, or All the Happy Places,
You Would Just See the Poverty Staring in Your Faces.

If You Could Touch this World, What Do You Think You'd Feel?
I Think You'd Feel the Harshness of the People Living Here,
You Wouldn't Feel the Tenderness, the Warmth or the Love,
You'd Just Feel the Harshness of the People Living Here.

Nicole Marie Angelique Brown
January 1994

Contents

Chapter 3 Children in Trouble   /67

Chapter 4 Parenting in the Jamaican Society   /91

Chapter 5 The Jamaican Child of the Nineties   /117

Foreword

This book breaks new ground for all who are interested in family life and child care in Jamaica. Thorough in analysis, Claudette Crawford-Brown does not shy away from prescriptive suggestions which should excite much-needed discourse and action among policy-makers, NGO activists and care-givers.

But more than this, the book is written with personal involvement and palpable compassion for those children who are deprived of love and of good care. The young ones cry out through these pages. The impact is to move the reader's heart as well as his or her head.

Ronald George Thwaites
July 1998

Preface

This book consists of a collection of reflective writings on issues affecting children in Jamaica in the 1990s and some implications for programme development and policy formulation. It uses material from the Children's Lobby column appearing in the Jamaica Herald between 1992 and 1994.

The book is written for use by teachers, nurses, social workers, planners, students and practitioners, as well as parents. It should prove useful to anyone who would like to get a sense of the direction in which the 1990s have taken us in terms of the social issues that are impacting on our children and families, and it seeks to point to those areas that need to be addressed in terms of research and effective programme and policy development.

In order to help the reader who wants to explore the topics in more detail, the book is organized so that at the end of each chapter there are guidelines as to the policy and research issues that need to be addressed, and there are specific suggestions about the ways in which these could be tackled at different levels of intervention. Each chapter also contains a list of resource material, which includes books, manuals and other reference material from the Caribbean and elsewhere that might prove useful to the reader who wants to know more about the particular issues discussed in the chapter. In addition, there is a general bibliography at the back of the book. Information on referral sources for the different problem areas is also included where appropriate.

A chapter on the Jamaican child welfare system is included at the beginning of the text. It examines and analyses some of the important macro systems issues which impact on the delivery of services for children who are wards of the state and who are in government care as a result of breakdown in their family units. This chapter begins with the diary of a nine year old child who passed through the Jamaican child welfare system. Written twenty years ago, the diary raises issues that are strikingly similar to these that impact on our present systems of service delivery. The second chapter, which focuses on children who need protection, looks at a range of circumstances in our society where children find themselves in need of protection. These include situations that could be described as being traditionally abusive, that is occurring within the family, as well as those situations where abuse occurs outside the home and which could be referred to as societal or institutional abuse. The third chapter titled Children Who Are in Trouble, examines the dilemma of children in difficulty with the law. It looks at some of the strategies that could be employed to get them out of their difficulties, by analyzing the factors that push children into criminal activity. The fourth chapter is a special one on parenting in the Jamaican society, the content of which is organized to facilitate easy reproduction. This is done to facilitate community based groups, such as parent- teachers associations (PTAs), youth clubs, and church groups, that can readily use this information to assist parents.

The final chapter, on the child in Jamaican society, is a summary of the book and looks at the reality of the lives of Jamaican children in the 1990s. It comments on some of the new and old initiatives set up to meet their needs, and points to the obstacles to their effectiveness. This chapter ends with a plea for intervention to help the Jamaican child, written and presented by two ten year old children, at the Inaugural Children's Lobby Awards for Child Advocates in Jamaica in May 1994.

Abbreviations

ACCE   -   Association of Child Care Employees

AWOJA   -   Association of Women's Organizations in Jamaica

CANSAVE   -   Canadian Save the Children Fund

CSD   -   Children's Services Division

CSU   -   Child Support Unit

CVSS   -   Council of Voluntary Social Services

JTA   -   Jamaica Teachers Association

MADD   -   Mothers Against Drunk Driving

NGO   -   Non-Governmental Organization

PICK   -   Parents of Inner-city Kids

PIOJ   -   Planning Institute of Jamaica

PSOJ   -   Private Sector Organization of Jamaica

POS   -   Place of Safety

UNICEF   -   United Nations International Children's Education Fund

VOUCH   -   Voluntary Organization for the Upliftment of Children

1

The Jamaican Child Welfare System

INTRODUCTION

The Role of Child Welfare in Society

Children are not safe and happy if their parents are miserable, and parents must be miserable if they cannot protect a home from poverty. Let us not deceive ourselves; The power to maintain a decent living standard is the primary essential of child welfare. (Julia Lathrop)[1]

The rationale for a modern child welfare system is based on the fact that the human child is unique and experiences a prolonged period of dependence on adult care, for support and guidance. This is provided by the child's family, either both parents or one parent. When there is family breakdown, however, this care is provided by extended family members (for example, grandparents). However, over several decades, due to sociocultural and economic changes, many societies, including those in the Caribbean, have had to offer this back up function by setting up organized societal institutions to provide this alternative form of care through child welfare systems (Kadushin 1967). Child welfare systems function through various social agencies in the government, as well as in the non-government sector, to provide alternative care for children, as it is assumed that they are not intellectually, emotionally or physically able to care for themselves. It is therefore accepted that society has a responsibility to care for its children when there is no one else.

Background to the Jamaican Social Welfare Situation

During the 1970s Jamaica weathered serious economic crises which were followed by harsh structural adjustment programmes. The reality of the Jamaican social welfare situation is that 39.8 percent of Jamaican children under 14 years (approximately 316,968 children) are in extreme poverty. In 1994, this was manifested by the fact that approximately 23,000 children between the ages of 6 and 16 years were classified as working children. Of this number 2,500 could be considered to be children of the streets and could be classified as homeless. In 1994, 81 children were classified as having some form of disability, and 3,000 children were resident in private and public children's homes (UNICEF 1986).

Demographic Factors

The most recent *Survey of Living Conditions* (Planning Institute of Jamaica 1995a) indicates that approximately 50 percent of the Jamaican population is under 18 years and approximately a third of this number are under 15 years. It is interesting to note that during the period 1988-1993, there was a 7.5 percent increase in the under five population, which now represents 11.5 percent of the total population. This has implications for planning child welfare policies and programmes, which must take these facts into account.

Poverty in Jamaica

In 1994 the unemployment rate among males was 9.6 percent and among females it was 21.8 percent, with the poorest 20 percent of the Jamaican population accounting for 6.5 percent of national consumption. Although the rates of unemployment in Jamaica fell from 27.6 percent in 1989 to 15.4 percent in 1994, the Planning Institute of Jamaica (PIOJ) reports that the quality of jobs deteriorated over the period. Though all poor households record at least one person unemployed, the 1995 *Survey of Living Conditions* confirms that many persons who are employed lack the required skills and so are confined to low productivity, low paying jobs. When there is poverty of this nature it is the children who are the most vulnerable group, in terms of its effect on their general welfare (Sabatini and Newman-Williams 1997). In a discussion of the 1996 National Plan of Action for Children, one PIOJ report describes poverty in Jamaica as an issue of the working poor rather than an issue of unemployment. The report suggests that most of the children who are from low income families experience varying degrees of deprivation in terms of a lack of intellectual stimulation and decreased levels of family stability, particularly in the first few years of their lives (PIOJ 1995b). The result is that many of our children end up living in extremely difficult situations and circumstances which put them at risk in terms of the quality of their lives, and the society has few mechanisms to ensure that there is an adequate safety net for their protection.

Inadequate Social Service Delivery

By the end of the 1980s it became evident to social planners and social practitioners that the overall social situation in Jamaica was such that the social services were no longer adequate to provide support to children and families in difficulty. The Children's Services Division (the main government agency responsible for providing services to children in especially difficult circumstances) was then the responsibility of the Ministry of Youth and it had been historically underfunded and understaffed. This agency had, and continues to have, the legal responsibility for children in need of care and protection in children's homes and places of safety. These children are usually the victims of family breakdown due to the deaths of parents or guardians, economic difficulties, migration, child abuse and abandonment. Some of these children are also in need of care and protection by virtue of the fact that their families deem them to be uncontrollable and so they are placed in government care. The behaviour of these children is assumed to be evidence that their families are unable to fulfill their parental function. In 1986-1987 the number of child care and protection cases coming before the Family Courts in Kingston and Montego Bay increased by 37.7 percent, from 1,693 to 2,331 (Planning Institute of Jamaica 1992). Though there has been a steady increase in the number of children needing care, over the years there continues to be cutbacks in funding, and so the agency that is the main government administrative body in charge of child welfare has never been given the attention it deserves. This has undoubtedly affected its efficiency and its effectiveness over the years. This chapter looks at some of the major problems facing this agency and suggests ways in which these problems can be addressed in a meaningful way.

FACTS CONCERNING CHILDREN IN GOVERNMENT CARE

There are four major types of alternative child care services available in Jamaica for children who are in need of care and protection: (1) children's homes, (2) foster care homes, (3) places of safety, and (4) adoption services.

In a survey of child care institutions in December 1993 there were 48 residential institutions (children's homes and places of safety) islandwide. Of these, 42 percent were located in Kingston and St Andrew. Of the total of 48 institutions there were 13 places of safety (9 government owned and 4 privately owned) and there were 35 children's homes, 28 of these being privately owned. These institutions at that time cared for just over 2,000 children. This represented 40.6 percent of the total number of children in care. Of this number 1,463 children (36 percent) were in children's homes (see Figure 1.1).

Disposition of Other Children in the System

In looking at the disposition of the other children in the system there were an additional 25 percent in foster care and 38 percent in places of safety. It is to be noted that the number of children in places of safety approximates the number of children in children's homes in the corporate area. This has

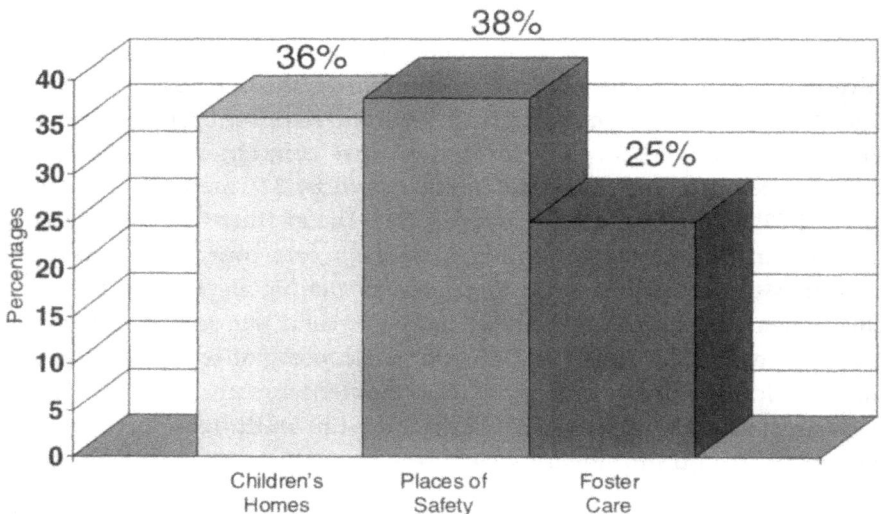

Fig. 1.1: Breakdown of Children in Alternative Care by Type, Corporate Area

serious implications for the role of places of safety, as they are not designed to cater to such large numbers of children in terms of meeting their psychological, intellectual and physical needs. Other systems of alternative care examined showed that 485 children were home on trial[2] and 1,417 were home on supervision orders.[3] (It is to be noted that children who are home on trial or on supervision orders often do not receive the required level of supervision, due to staff shortages and other resource problems.)

The total number of children in the social welfare system at December 1992 was 3,941, ranging in age from birth to 18 years. Given the number of children to be served, the lack of resources in the system, as well as its complexity, there are a number of immediate problems facing the Children's Services Division.

Age Range of the Children

In one small study done in 1993 on urban residential child care institutions (Patterson and Wood 1993), it was determined that the age pattern of the children created certain problems, as the single largest group (25 percent) represented in the system was under six years old, with 5 percent of them under one year old (see Figure 1.2). This is of some importance in terms of resource allocation, as staff/child ratios should be higher for this age group.

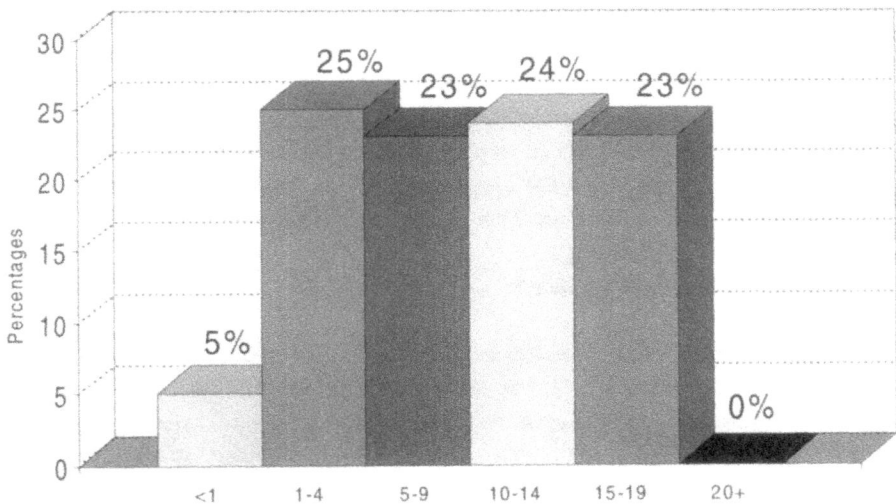

Fig. 1.2: Distribution of Children in Alternative Child Care Arrangements, Corporate Area

Sex Ratio of Children

The 1993 study reported that a slightly higher percentage of boys were represented in the sample of institutionalized children (52.7 percent of the children were boys, 47.3 percent were girls). Historically, boys have represented the greater proportion of children in care. This could relate to the fact that boys are perceived to "give more trouble", and are seen as being harder to manage (Brodber 1972; Levy and Chevannes 1996) than girls, so they are placed in government care more readily.

Factors Bringing Children Into Care

Abandonment can be described as the worst form of neglect and the 1993 report suggested that this was the biggest factor causing children to be brought into care, with the majority of these children being in the 0-5 year age group (see Table 1.1). Of the total children in care investigated, the study found that 54.4 percent came into the system due to abandonment or neglect. Over 16 percent (16.6 percent) of them were in the system due to behavioral problems, and 14 percent of them came into care as a result of stated economic factors (it is to be noted that economic factors could also have caused abandonment). The other 15 percent were there for a variety of other problems and 7.7 percent were there as a result of physical or sexual abuse.

Knowledge of trends in data such as this, provided annually or every two years, would go a far way to help planners to understand the factors pushing children into the system. This would enable them to do solution-based programme development. If, for example, our largest group of children brought into care have been abandoned, this could be tackled through prevention and public education programmes for families. Providing families with some economic support to enable them to keep their infants could go a far way in cutting down on the large numbers of children coming in due to abandonment by their families. Thus, scarce resources could be better utilized.

Specialized Intervention Needs

There are also hundreds of children who need stimulation and well developed educational programmes suited to their developmental as well as their social and psychological needs. Some children need therapeutic services to help them to cope with their sometimes overwhelming feelings: of abandonment and rejection, as well as feelings related to separation from parents and family, which are often acted out as hostility and aggression. Others suffer from low self esteem as a result of constant physical or sexual abuse as well

Table 1.1
Showing Reasons Why Children Are In Care
1991-1992 (Children's Homes and Places of Safety Kingston and St. Andrew)

Factors Causing Admission	INSTITUTIONS*																			
	A		B		C		D		E		F		G		H		I		Total	
	No.	%	No.	%	No.	%	No.	%	No.	%	No.	%	No.	%	No.	%	No.	%	No.	%
Abandonment /Neglect**	43	80	21	43	24	47	13	27	23	31	32	72	18	53	42	82	18	48	225	54.4
Child Abuse (Physical & Sexual)	-	-	7	15	-	-	11	23	7	9	8	20	-	-	-	-	-	-	33	7.7
Economic Factor	-	-	13	27	11	23	4	9	5	6	2	4	12	33	2	5	11	29	60	14
Behaviour Factors	9	20	7	15	11	23	17	36	18	24	2	4	7	7	-	-	5	14	71	16.6
Children with Disabilities	-	-	-	-	4	7	2	5	22	30	-	-	2	7	7	13	3	9	40	9.3
Total	43		48		50		47		75		44		34		51		37		429	

* INSTITUTIONS represent places of safety and children's homes in the corporate area.
**The majority of children in this category (70%) were aged 0-6.

as institutional abuse from untrained staff. Many others, particularly those abandoned since birth, just long to have the support of (and to experience what it is like to have) a family.

PROBLEMS OF JAMAICAN CHILD WELFARE

Jamaican society has often been described as a friendly, caring and loving one, and we all say we love our children. However, there are a number of children who regularly fall through the cracks of our social service systems. These children are often described as disadvantaged. They are the abandoned, the abused, the neglected children described above, and the ones who "give trouble". Our children's homes and places of safety are full of these children. They are the real casualties of the structural adjustment programmes and other socioeconomic changes that have taken place in our society since the 1970s.

From time to time we hear news reports about their problems and the concerns of these disadvantaged children. However, over the past two decades their basic conditions have remained unchanged. Who really are these children? Why do they continue to have problems year after year? How does the agency responsible for their care cope with these problems and what can we as a society do to help them? One of the major obstacles that prevent us from answering these questions is the lack of an efficient system in the main children's service agency from which basic data can be recorded and disseminated. This leads to a situation in which the society seems to be unaware of the full nature of the work of the agency or the extent of its function. The Children's Services Division is presumably the easiest to cut, and the last to receive additional funding in so-called "boom times", as there is a lack of data to justify its existence and relevance to the economy.

The ongoing difficulties of the agency include a lack of adequate funds for efficient management and operation of a national child welfare system, the absence of well developed training programmes, as well as the nature of the agency's present structure and function, which is oriented to custodial rather than therapeutic care. The agency therefore has a range of problems which must be addressed if there is to be effective child welfare reform. These problems, however, have existed for some time, as documented below.

The Diary of a Child in Care

Some of the problems experienced within the children's service agency are clearly illustrated in the words of a thirteen year old child in care who wrote of her experiences in the Jamaican child welfare system in a diary over twenty years ago. Her words are recorded below. (The report is presented in its original form except for those instances where the original words would make it difficult to understand.)

The excerpt is enlightening to the extent that it highlights the problems that currently beset the child welfare system. The original names of the individuals were changed to protect their privacy.

I was born in 1961. I am 9 years old. I am short and fat but not that fat. I have a very nice complexion and I am very pretty according to peoples. I have two sisters and one brother. I like them very much. One of my sister is 8 years old that is my little sister and my biggest sister is 16 years old. My brother is 10 years old. And I am 9 years old as I told you before. There are four of us. We live loving. I don't say that we don't have a little fuss but that we have to sometimes you know that. But anyway let us jump to the conclusions. We was living with our mother and father, that is the first day I was born and see, that I was living with them. Any way I was 4 years old when I know myself. From I was coming up I always see my father beating my mother. He use to beat her very badly, I don't like when he is beating her, he kick her and box her and do all the things you know is bad. We use to live in a little house. I don't know who the house belong to but we live in it. I was telling you about my father what he did. Why he did all these things is because he got my mother pregnant and he don't want her anymore. He tell her to leave him alone and come out of his house. He beat her as I tell you before and she still keep on staying there so I said to her "Mama why don't you come out of his house and leave him alone". She look at me and then pick me up and put me in her lap and put her hands around my neck. She start to cry. I feel sorry for her. Then she said "you know that mama don't have anywhere to go". So I said "then can we go up to his relatives and she said that they would run her. Then she put me down and started to pack and then when it was evening she leave. I did not know where she went. I know she leave. And then I find myself on the street sleeping that night. I did not say anything to my mother like what we are doing here? I went back to sleep.

The next day she get up very early and wake us up and give us tea. I don't know where she get it because I know she did not have any money. Anyway I eat it. I was intend to ask her, but I think she will say I ask too much questions. Then we began to walk and walk like I never walk before. Then we came to a house and I see a lady was watering and my mother ask her for a drink of water, then we sat and drink the water and start to walk again. Then I see my mother walk up to this black gate. I ask her if she is going to ask for something to eat again, because they will run her this time. She said no! she is going into the house. I ask her if she know the people and she said yes. Then I did not hear what she said to the lady. But she just went in and we went in with her in a room. I see a bed, a big bed and two chairs. I ask if she is going to live there and she said yes. I said I do not like the place and she smile and said "Is not what you want you get Dee-Dee". My name is Donna but she shorted it and call me Dee-Dee. Anyway I said you are right Mama. She smile and put her hand around my neck. I smile too.

Then we start to unpack and make up the bed and so. We live about 6 months. We could stay there long but something happen. Me and my sister and brother was playing under the table, we was playing bus driver. Anyway my brother was the driver. Some oil was under the table and my brother drink it off, all of it. It was kerosene-oil and then he said "I feel nice", and we started to laugh, and my brother start to drive again. All of a sudden I see my brother stop driving and he fell on the floor. I run out and call Mama and tell her something happen to Bas. We use to call him Bas as a nickname. My mother run inside and pick him up and start to cry, she said what happen to him? I said he drink the oil and she said "What?" She hurry up and put on his clothes and run out of the house and hurry down the road. I started to cry because I did not know what was the danger. Anyway I lock up the door and stay inside, me and my sister that was the big one. Oh let me tell you something about her, she do things that is out of the way. She cannot read or write. She is sick, she has epilepsy every day that God send. When she has it her eyes turn over. I have to put a spoon over her mouth. Anyway we was looking for our mother to come. We wait and wait and still we don't see her. Then my sister said let us to go bed. I agreed with her and I go to bed. I did not know when I fell asleep. The next morning I was waked by a knock at the door and I wake up my sister and tell her that Mama come and to my surprise I see the lady for the rent. I told her my mother was not here right now. I don't know when she is coming back. Just as I done talking I see her at the gate with a very sad face. I run to meet her. I ask her what the doctor said is going to happen to Bas and she said that the doctor said that he is not going to live, and I was shocked. I could not move then she said that she can come for him the next day. I did not sleep that night I just kept on thinking on my brother. The next morning my mother heard someone knock at the gate and my mother said I should went outside to see who was it. I see that it was my father. I said that Mama don't want to see you and we don't want to see you, and same time my mother came up and said that I must go inside. I hear what she said and I go inside and the two of them started to talk. I did not know what they were talking about. Then I see my father put his hands around my mother neck and kiss her and the two of them come in the house and they said to me that my father is staying with us. I said that I don't want him to stay and my mother ask me why? I said because he is going to beat you up again and she said "no he promised he will never hit me again". I did not believe my father. Then I said, the woman that he have must eat out him money and leave him. Is who tell me to say that? He just open his hand and box me across my face. My mother did not like that but she said Dee-Dee you must not say that. He was about to give me another one and my mother stop him and said to him "She is little, she don't know what she is saying". Then they walk off and leave me, I started to cry. I know what I was saying, you yourself would say the same thing. They live together now she was pregnant again. Then one day my father said he was going out and he will be soon come back. My mother cooked dinner for everyone. She gave us our dinner and left. My father dinner was on the table. I went to my bed. I did not know what was going on. I wake the next morning and saw my mother and ask her where was my father and she said he did not come home last night. I was glad he is not coming back home. He did not come because he know that he got my mother pregnant again. I am sorry to say this but I think that my mother is a fool. She just make a man make a fool out of her don't you think so? It was the last baby she was going to have that was my last sister. Then one day the lady for the house said to my mother "you have three children why do you have to get more. I do not like many children in my house". Then my mother said to the lady "it is none of your business". Then the lady start to quarrel with my mother, I did not butt into it because I know they would put me in my place. The next day my mother leave. I was on the street again, boy it was so bad to see us on the street. Then we go on with the same things too. Then we was living with another lady, her name was Miss Edwards. She did not married but she has four children. I did not like her because she never want her children to play with us. I give her a funny name, a very funny name. The name was "Wash-Wash". From I call her that name everyone call her that every time. When we play with her children she always call them inside. One day she was bathing one of them, she was bathing the boy. Then she said to him did I tell you not to play with the children and he said yes but they are my friends, then she said I will see if they are your friends and she went for the belt and started to beat him in the bath for playing with us. Then she go to a house I did not know, the lady make we live there a whole month. I did not like there. One night my mother went to a party and she was dancing then she heard some quarreling and she went to see. By the time she reach she see a man stab another man in his chest and then she tell her friends to call the police. Then she grab me and my sister and brother and start to run. She run and jump over the dead man. I feel very sad for the dead man. Any way we run up the road. I ask her why she is running like that and she said that she don't want the police to ask her anything. Then she make us sleep on the road again. We get no food no nothing. The next day she went to a very old lady and she gave us food and so on and we live there for only two weeks. Then I see my mother moving again and she went up to the lady sister to stay and she got another job at last. This time she said she is not going to allow my father in there. I said you don't have to say that because he is not coming back. Don't you think I am right, he got what he want already don't you think so too? One day my mother was packing and I ask her where she was going. She said to the U S of A. She went for a taxi and she said everything was going to be all right for us. Then one day her sister came to the house and said that my mother is dead and my sister started to cry. I did not cry because I was shocked and I could not move. They put us at a place call foster home. We were not there long, about 100 or so children was there, I am not telling no lie. One hundred and twenty-five children. I did not like the place at all. The children some of them do-do and eat it back. They was starving. Many food was not there for them to get so that is why they do that. Then a lady come in a car and take us up to a pretty house. She own the house and her name was Miss Townsend....

The diary ended here. It was given to the author in 1976, with permission by the child to use it to help other children.

Dee-Dee and her siblings were taken into foster care. After several breakdowns in foster placements over a three year period, Dee-Dee and her siblings were placed in one of the best children's homes in the island, in a cottage-type setting. Throughout this period little contact was made with Dee-Dee's father or his family or her mother's family in an attempt to get these children back into their family of origin. When contact was made, the family expressed little interest and the system did not or could not mandate the family to assume responsibility. Dee-Dee and her siblings attended school in the community and seemed well adjusted. They were very friendly and happy, but as Dee-Dee approached the age of seventeen it was discovered that she was pregnant. Dee-Dee stated that against her wishes she was forced to have an abortion. The operation was botched and Dee-Dee became sterile. Dee-Dee returned to live with her father at age eighteen, when she was no longer a ward of the state. Her father, on realizing that Dee-Dee could not conceive, put her out on the streets to "look it" and thus began her first career as a prostitute.

Lessons Learnt From the Diary

This diary is a graphic illustration of the kinds of problems that push children into care, and the kinds of situations that prompt family dissolution, such as migration, spousal abuse, female dependence, lack of housing, disabilities, lack of supervision, community violence and accidents. The diary speaks to the impressions of the child welfare system from a child's point of view. It documents the anxiety that children experience when they go to court and go through all the different processes within the child welfare system. The fact that very often no one explains to children why they go from one place to the next, or what is happening to them, is illustrated. The answers to such questions as "Why are they in care?", "How long will they be there?", "What is happening to them and why?" are not considered important information to be communicated to the children. Sometimes siblings are separated from each other and no one tells them why or tries to maintain communication between them. Child welfare reform must address these issues urgently if we are to offer a meaningful service to children and families, that meets their basic needs.

Need to be "Child-friendly"

This report, taken directly from the child's point of view, illustrates the need to build "child-friendly" operations into the existing child welfare system. Developing a national children's policy, as was recently done in Jamaica, is only a first step. Every aspect of programming should reflect child-friendly policies. This diary also speaks to the insensitivity of individuals and agencies within the child welfare system almost 20 years ago. Though some of the physical conditions have changed (the specific children's institution in which this child was placed has since been closed by the authorities), the basic policies which cause children to be shifted from one foster home to another, to their detriment, still remain. As a consequence, there is no system of *permanency planning* built into foster care, and therefore there is little concept of long-range planning, to assure for each child some stability, particularly in his or her important early school-age and middle school-age years. (The concept of permanency planning ensures that foster parents commit themselves to specific periods of care. During that time children cannot be returned to the child welfare agency.) When, in addition, there is little use of treatment plans, and an efficient system of adoptive care does not support the child welfare system, the entire system must be described as having serious shortcomings. There has been little movement in the child welfare system towards modern policies and programmes over the past twenty years, since the diary was written. It still serves to highlight some of the most glaring deficiencies of the Jamaican child welfare system, particularly as it relates to direct intervention with the child and family.

Lack of Prevention Programmes

An agency working with children in difficult circumstances must put in place intensive prevention programmes to ensure that children do not have to end up in institutions, outside of their families of origin. Families can be empowered and supported to enable them to keep their children. This kind of intervention will prevent family breakdown and will go a long way to reducing expenditure in the long term, as long term institutionalization is an expensive method of child care. One of the issues that was highlighted in Dee Dee's diary was the need for family support and social service intervention at a much earlier stage. Intervention before breakdown could have saved this family; early intervention could have saved this child; early intervention could have saved a life now wasted.

It is interesting to note that the Children's Services Division is ideally placed to have an impact on the prevention of a wide range of problems affecting children in the home and community. Succeeding government administrations have made important investments in an agency like this by awarding undergraduate and graduate scholarships to agency personnel for training in social work and related fields at universities here and abroad. A significant part of the problem is that, although training is adapted to the needs of Caribbean societies, graduates are often reluctant to go back to an agency that is not using modern management and intervention techniques that are normal for their discipline in the twentieth century, and one where in-house training is ad hoc rather than integral to the agency's operation. A child welfare agency that is not equipped with a trained research or data collection officer, or one that is not guided by a well thought out policy framework, will have problems interfacing with most of the other social and economic service sectors in the society. In the Ministry of Health, for example, performance in certain areas of the health sector in recent years has been worthy of national and international commendation, especially in relation to the degree of immunization coverage. The Ministry of Health is a powerful ministry with good technical strength at the highest levels of its administration. Similarly, the Ministry of Education is well endowed with professionals at the highest levels of its administration, who plan and direct programmes and policies for the education sector. The Children's Services Division with the Ministry of Health must be given the necessary clout and human resources, in the form of well-trained social work professionals, to effectively manage the affairs of our children who are in especially difficult circumstances, at the highest levels of government administration.

Territorialism

The diary, written so many years ago, also points to the fact that there is a need for agencies working with children to devise a mechanism to work together through a system of effective case management, and through the use of case conferences, to ensure that they work in the best interest of the children who come into care. This means that the schools, the non-governmental organizations (NGOs) working with children, and the main children service agencies must work together in the best interest of each child.

Need for Increased Child Advocacy

It is now twenty years since this diary was written. The time is ripe for real and effective advocacy for our children. We have to shed the old ways of doing things, including the colonial "divide and rule" policy which has led to so much territorialism among our social service agencies. We must collaborate, respect each other's differences, and realize that Jamaica is changing rapidly. The fact is that other sectors of our society are benefiting from the synergies of sharing information. It should be just as easy, or maybe even easier, for child welfare agencies to do the same, since the nature of our work is implicitly collaborative and not competitive. We have a job to do on behalf of our children. We must work not only to improve service delivery, but we must understand the need to do this through relentless advocacy on their behalf, with a sustained and united voice. It is not enough to participate in promoting children's rights during Child Month.[4] Children's agencies must work together on behalf of children, throughout the year, to promote and push for meaningful change, lest our children lose faith in us.

POLICY ON CHILD WELFARE

A national policy stating the basic principles upon which the children welfare system should function, as well as an operational policy for children in care that is readily available and accessible to the professionals in the system, is one of the most urgent needs facing Jamaican child welfare. Given the historical weakness of the child welfare system to effect change, however, there is need for heightened and sustained advocacy to support this policy development effort within the agencies concerned.

The Role of Advocacy in Policy Development

There are a number of issues which over the years keep cropping up in the press and in conferences and seminars on children in Jamaica. Agencies and organizations such as the Council of Voluntary Social Services (CVSS), the Voluntary Organization for the Upliftment of Children (VOUCH), the Jamaica Association of Social Workers, the Jamaica Coalition on the Rights of the Child, and the Children's Lobby have been making appeals and pronouncements, for years, asking for certain basic components to be put in place to improve the conditions affecting our children. These basic components include the development of a comprehensive policy on children and the establishment of a national database for children.

A comprehensive policy should set the framework for meaningful change for our children, and a national database, which could be accessed by children's service agencies and other organizations, and allow government agencies to plan more effectively for children, would greatly enhance the effectiveness of the child welfare system.

Child advocacy groups in Jamaica have been calling for a national policy for children from as far back as 1986. During the International Year of the Child and since then, there has been a sustained cry. In 1996 a National Plan of Action (Planning Institute of Jamaica 1995b) and a National Policy for children were produced, but the information they contain is still largely unavailable to the practitioners who are supposed to implement them. The development of any social policy must be seen as a dynamic process, which changes constantly to meet the demands of the clients it is developed to serve. A policy for children must involve social workers and allied practitioners in its development. Now that one has been drafted by the Planning Institute of Jamaica, this policy must now be made public, discussed and amended where necessary if it is to be meaningful, effective and operational.

Integrated Children and Family Services

A policy for children in Jamaica must also tackle the issues of the integration of services for families and children and social welfare services. A policy for children must address the issue of the restructuring of services and programmes so that after careful assessment, disposition decisions can be made based on psychosocial factors; for example, children needing specialized treatment can be distinguished from those needing skills training, and small grants can be provided to specific families who are in need. This kind of programme and procedure must form part of a new preventive component of the Children's Services Division. Such a preventive programme would go a far way in eradicating the scourge of the abandonment of infants, the mass institutionalization of young children, as well as the flow of street children into the highways and byways of rural and urban Jamaica. The proposals that are put to government on these and other policy matters concerning children must, however, be done by consensus. They must involve a wide range of agencies, practitioners, advocacy groups and policy makers working with children so that they speak to government with one voice that is sustained and unwavering in its defense of this most vulnerable group in our society – the nation's children.

ADMINISTRATIVE REFORM OF SERVICES FOR CHILDREN

Children's Services in Jamaica: The Football of Succeeding Government Administrations

Government services to children have historically been characterized as the "football agency" of succeeding government administrations. Consequently, the agency has never really been taken seriously. It has been shunted from ministry to ministry and has never seemed to be an agency with a clear sense of where it is going. For several years, different administrations of the

Government of Jamaica have seen fit to move the Children's Services Division, the agency responsible for providing social services for children, from the Ministry of Youth to the Ministry of Local Government, to the Ministry of Health, where it now resides. This factor has by itself ensured a certain degree of instability as it relates to the capability of the agency to do any forward or long range planning, which would enable it to improve the quality and scope of its services. The offices assigned to this agency usually have the barest minimum in terms of office furniture and facilities and they have limited access at the central or regional level to other basic equipment such as photocopy machines, fax machines and computers, which are normal fixtures in similar offices in the Ministry of Health network and the Ministry of Education. The special needs of this agency, such as rooms for interviewing families and office partitions to ensure confidentiality, are also not considered as important in the allocation of resources to this agency.

In light of the fact that children are not voters, and in the absence of a well organized lobby over several decades, this agency has never been able to take its "rightful place" as the lead agency in charge of children and their families. If we are to deal effectively with the social problems and the social agenda for our people, this is one of the first agencies that must be made functional and effective.

When one looks at the history of child welfare services in Jamaica in terms of budget allocation patterns over the years, it is well documented that this particular area of the social services has always been the "Cinderella" of the government service. As a result agency staffers, though hard working, have low morale and there is a high rate of staff turnover. The agency itself has therefore traditionally been underfunded and understaffed.

On occasion, overall budgetary allocations were increased, but specific allocations to crucial sectors were cut. For example, there were instances where additional budgetary allocations were made to the Ministry of Youth. However, decreased sums were allocated to crucial sectors such as children's services (and) youth and community development (services) *(Economic and Social Survey Jamaica 1992).*

Staff Training

Most agencies providing welfare to children and families are not giving the necessary attention to upgrading the skill level of staff, and so new practice modalities are rarely introduced. As a result, many practitioners are not even aware that such concepts as permanency planning, family reunification or alternate family placements in the form of small group homes are viable child welfare strategies, and so these strategies are hardly, if ever, used in foster care planning. The concept of open adoption has hardly been discussed regarding its application in a small society such as ours. The use of art and play therapy in the assessment of young children, and the use of new therapies such as solution-focused therapy, which are some of the basic tools of the modern social work practitioner, have not yet been tried or discussed in most of our social service agencies working with children. It must be emphasized that those agencies working directly with children and their families in the NGO and government sectors need to develop and implement comprehensive staff training programmes on an ongoing basis. Such training programmes are an essential component of a modern organization, particularly a modern child welfare system. These training programmes should be both cumulative and modular in nature and should be instituted as a fundamental and necessary part of the functioning of the Children's Services and Correctional Services Divisions. The Correctional Services Division has for years been one of the few family based agencies that implements some in-service training. All children and family agencies should have systematic, coordinated and integrated in-service training programmes to ensure effective service delivery.

Modern Management Practices

If we look at the administration of our social services, particularly those serving the needs of children in the NGO and government sectors, we find that modern management practices are not as commonplace as they should be, and computers, for example, are still seen only as a tool for word processing. There are several simple computer-based applications for the assessment of children and families that can be used by agencies working with children and families, which are yet untapped by most of our agencies. Most of these agencies are unaware of the utility of these computer applications and other tools, such as computer networking for information dissemination, which are widely available in the modern social service agency.

Computerized Communication Systems

The possibilities for increased efficiency and effectiveness in the child welfare system are tremendous if the agencies could work together to develop a network of information using the various databases on the children with whom they work. This network needs to be developed across the country, as well as within the Caribbean region. Access to information systems outside of the Caribbean is also essential to avoid reinventing the wheel, so that we can avoid duplication of effort and maximize the use of the technology available to us. Through the Internet, vital information is readily available. Our tertiary institutions can readily access this kind of information and make it available to the agencies through electronic community bulletin boards which are strategic, simple and inexpensive to establish. The NGO community serving children would be a good place to start to establish such a network.

Organizational Restructuring: Health Care Needs vs. Child Welfare Needs

The repeated concerns expressed in this publication suggest that there is need for a level of technical expertise in child welfare in the Health Ministry which is not currently available. This expertise is needed above the level of chief children's officer and is necessary to balance the technical expertise presently exhibited by the health professionals currently in charge of the medical aspects of the administration of the Ministry of Health. For example, could there be a senior technical officer with specific responsibility for children's services, who would then have the administrative clout to push through legislative and other changes to make the children's agency more effective? The worrisome thought concerning the future of the Children's Services Division and the Child Support Unit (which has so much potential as a policy development unit), now under the Ministry of Health, is that the well articulated needs of the health sector will be the ones that will be put forward for receipt of the few resources available for the social services, and the urgent needs of the traditional children's welfare services will not receive the attention they deserve. The obvious danger is that the child welfare sector may become subsumed under health planning and programming, without sufficient attention being paid to the specific programmatic needs of the sector. The child welfare sector has its own special needs and professional dictates which are closely related to the social work profession and allied professions such as family therapy and clinical psychology. In any effective system of social service delivery to children, it is of paramount importance to examine the root causes within the family, and to establish well thought out prevention programmes implemented by a highly trained cadre of children and family service practitioners, administered by an efficient and modern child welfare agency. The reality is that without such a system, we will be lamenting the tragedy of our abused children, street children and other serious child-related problems for years to come. We cannot continue to deny the children's service agencies the political or technical support from the top and we cannot continue to give the children's service officers the proverbial baskets to carry water.

The facts presented above suggest specific solutions and recommendations for dealing with problems in the child welfare system, which are summarized below.

SOLUTIONS AND RECOMMENDATIONS

Efficient recording system – There is need for an efficient recording system, computerized if possible, to ensure that children can be located and/or tracked through the child welfare system, so that the Children's Services Division can more efficiently contribute, via research and documentation, to national policy and planning for children.

Community sponsorship programmes – Well developed and well marketed sponsorship programmes patterning some of the international children's sponsorship programmes in Africa and South America could be used to supplement the limited resources of the Children's Services Division. Such programmes would target working and middle class families who could sponsor these children either in their own families and/or in institutions. Sponsors could be given progress reports on the children, and children could keep in touch with their sponsors by letters and other media. Sponsors would not attempt to supplant the role of the family and could be anonymous.

Public education for effective programme management – The case of alternative care (foster care and adoption services) is an underutilized aspect of the present child welfare system. The present situation is that there are not enough parents who are adequately prepared for the job. There are not enough genuine or well trained foster parents or adoptive parents. In order for a child welfare system to function effectively and efficiently, all alternative and supportive parenting programmes, such as foster care, home on trial, supervision and adoptive programmes must be vibrant and well managed, and they must have an ongoing and dynamic training and support programme for parents. Some potential foster parents in our culture, for example, often see the children in care as "mini-helpers". There is need for an ongoing public relations programme within the Children's Services Division, to sensitize the society to the needs of disadvantaged children. There should be special emphasis on intensive orientation and ongoing training in the foster care programme. In order to attract new foster parents, each week a case study of a needy child could be highlighted in the electronic or print media. Foster care is an important channel of the child care system which could move children out of institutions and into homes (see Figure 1.3). An expanded foster care programme would need

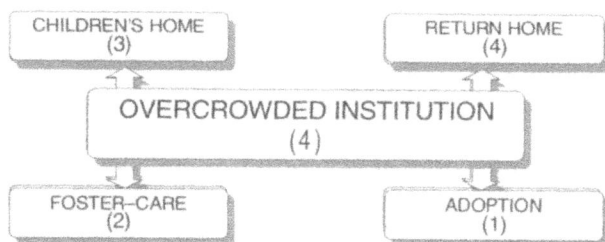

CHILDREN'S HOME
(3)

RETURN HOME
(4)

OVERCROWDED INSTITUTION
(4)

FOSTER-CARE
(2)

ADOPTION
(1)

Fig. 1.3 Showing Channels of Exit from the Places of Safety for Child in Need of Care and Protection

important training inputs as well as monetary resources for parents. Pooled resources in the form of central skills training centres for children in care in a particular region, for example, with complementary counselling programmes, could assist the limited resources of foster parents. These are projects that can be supplemented by private sector and service club involvement in the rural areas. It is important to note that these facilities already exist in the urban areas, but are largely underutilized.[5]

Special needs of infants – There must be a basic policy stipulating that infants and young children should not be institutionalized, as far as possible, except in extreme cases where this is the *only* viable option. Over forty years of research (Bowlby 1965) in child development has consistently found that institutionalization is the most traumatic way to care for young children. The preferred alternatives of adoption and foster care services need to be upgraded and conscientiously managed in order to be effective. It is possible that this may only work efficiently if these services are privatized, and we may want to be thinking along these lines, as a country, to examine these options and make clear decisions about the management of the entire child welfare system in terms of what is in the best interest of our children.

Rationalization of existing institutions – There needs to be a rationalization of the existing child care institutions to determine which institutions are best suited for the special needs of children. For example, should some institutions specialize in therapeutic services for the more disturbed children, while others focus on vocational and rehabilitation services? In a society with limited resources these are some of the concerns that must be addressed.

Rationalization of all agencies working for children – The future of different government and non-government groups and bodies working with and on behalf of the child must be clearly delineated to ensure a minimum of duplication and overlapping so as to enhance efficiency in meeting the needs of our children. There must be clear lines of referral, so that all agencies see themselves as a team working towards a common goal rather than crabs in a barrel, fighting for the scarce local and international funding that is available, guiding their turf zealously as if at war. The Child Support Unit could be responsible for the coordination and monitoring of these agencies in association with the CVSS.

Training and intervention – The upgrading, retooling, and ongoing training of institutional staff for children's homes and places of safety must be given priority, with strict and clear performance standards and job descriptions for difference levels of staff. Though there have been some improvements in this area, there are still large numbers of caring staff in these institutions who remain untrained and see themselves as providing only custodial care. The reopening of the National Children's Home as a training institution must be followed through. Quality care must be provided for these children as a real alternative to their homes or else they should be returned to their families. The institutions should move to the stage where each region or zone has access, at prescribed intervals, to a trained postgraduate social work practitioner or psychologists as part of a team responsible not just for reinforcing administrative policy, but also for training and supervision of clinical child care workers and children's officers who are working with children and their families. The task of this team would be to help children's officers move the children back into their homes where they belong, thus freeing up the system. Moving the child away from home permanently is not always the best solution and it is the most expensive.

Deinstitutionalization – If services are to be deinstitutionalized there must first be a careful assessment of the existing facilities with a delineation of their strengths and weaknesses, as was done in the decade-old study of institutions by Semaj and Redfearn (1988). It is to be noted, however, that the assessment of institutions cannot be a one-shot research activity, but must be done annually so that one can evaluate the institution's programmes and their effectiveness in terms of meeting the needs of children. There must be viable community alternatives in place to provide for these children in terms of resources, such as trained family workers, and proper policy development and plans at the national and community levels. The human resources for effective policy development are available in the society through NGOs and other institutions at minimal cost to the government agencies. The children's services must be helped to make use of these resources so that the agency can move into the twenty-first century properly equipped to deal with a whole new set of problems ahead, such as AIDS, child prostitution, child labour and 'hard' drug addiction and abuse.

Advocacy for children - The need to develop and sustain strong advocacy groups for children is critical in order to keep children's issues on the front burner of government policy. This can be done within the existing NGO framework, but with the impending pull out of international funding from the traditional United Nations agencies, there may be need for government assistance to strengthen these groups in the same way that the national consumer groups receive small government subventions.

Lobbying through parliamentary fora - There is need to push for the establishment of parliamentary hearings during which different lobby groups for children can present research and plans on behalf of women and children. Having children commenting on the National Children's Policy in the Jamaican Parliament in 1996 was one strategy, but the policy makers were for the most part amused and did not take the children seriously, in terms of long term and fundamental change. In addition to the use of child participation as a strategy, ongoing decision making on children's issues must be put into the hands of practitioners and planners who work with these children. These practitioners must equip themselves with the skills to rise to this challenge through diligent research using, where possible, the children themselves. The Children's Parliament project should not be a one-shot activity set up for the amusement of policy makers without diligent follow-up. The use of children to advocate on their own behalf should be institutionalized as part of the permanent strategy of advocacy groups, and should not be seen as a "cute" one-time activity. Children's voices can be made to be a powerful tool in the child advocacy effort and should not be seen as a gimmick.

As a society we must understand that caring for all of our children, regardless of their circumstances, is a concern born out of self preservation. Disadvantaged children today produce deviance and pathology tomorrow. One of the most important tasks that any responsible and mature society must undertake, if it is to count itself as civilized, is the care of this most vulnerable population. Taking care means diligence, commitment and taking a stand when something is obviously going wrong. We have to stop pointing fingers at each other and do something ourselves to amplify the voices that speak on behalf of the Jamaican child. This question of advocacy must be seen from the perspective of its relationship to policy development. However, the link between these two forces has not been taken seriously in Jamaica to date, and is one of those areas that need to be addressed urgently in the quest for meaningful child welfare reform.

SUMMARY

This chapter suggests that for years the existing system of child welfare (one of the legacies of the old British colonial social service system) has relied on mass institutionalization as the major method of providing alternative care for children when there is family breakdown. The Jamaican child welfare system, however, has not kept up with the times (Cumper 1972). There have been few attempts to evaluate its effectiveness, and even fewer attempts over the years to look at global systems, strategies, and methods of intervention, in order to evaluate its functioning in terms of the needs of Jamaica and the rest of the Caribbean. The result is an antiquated system which is not meeting the needs of the clients it was designed to serve, providing mainly custodial rather than therapeutic or preventive services. For example, in a system where over 2,000 children are placed in government care annually, less than 5 percent of those children receive any form of preliminary or ongoing assessment of their emotional and/or psychological state by their primary care giver (Planning Institute of Jamaica 1995c). Such assessments are absolutely essential for children who have experienced emotional trauma due to abandonment, violence and other forms of abuse and neglect. They are also important as planning tools and as a means of helping them to achieve greater levels of functioning as children, as well as later on as adults who themselves will become parents. The basic factors affecting social service delivery to these children relate to the fact that the agency looking after their needs is one of relatively low status in succeeding government administrations, being the first one to receive budget cuts, and the last one to receive increases in funding.

As a consequence, various policy makers have not treated the agency with the importance it deserves, and policy formulation for children and children's issues has been characterized by fragmentation and a lack of consistency from one administration to the next. In a presentation at the first Children's Lobby Conference of Child Advocates in 1986, entitled "The Social Status of the Jamaican Child", Dr. Edwin Jones of the Department of Government, University of the West Indies, suggested that historically, children's policies in Jamaica have been instituted without any empirical foundation, and policy development efforts have been scattered throughout the different agencies of government. This is still the situation ten years later. In addition, programmes are implemented with little, if any, input from the practitioners who are expected to work on these programmes and are usually instituted in response to one crisis or another by politicians, most of whom have very little training in the area of child welfare management or practice.

This chapter offers suggestions for solutions in terms of restructuring the child welfare system to include preventive services, protective services, alternate care services, and research and evaluation components (see Figure 1.4). Such a structure would emphasize direct intervention with families for both the prevention and intervention services components. Ideas were offered

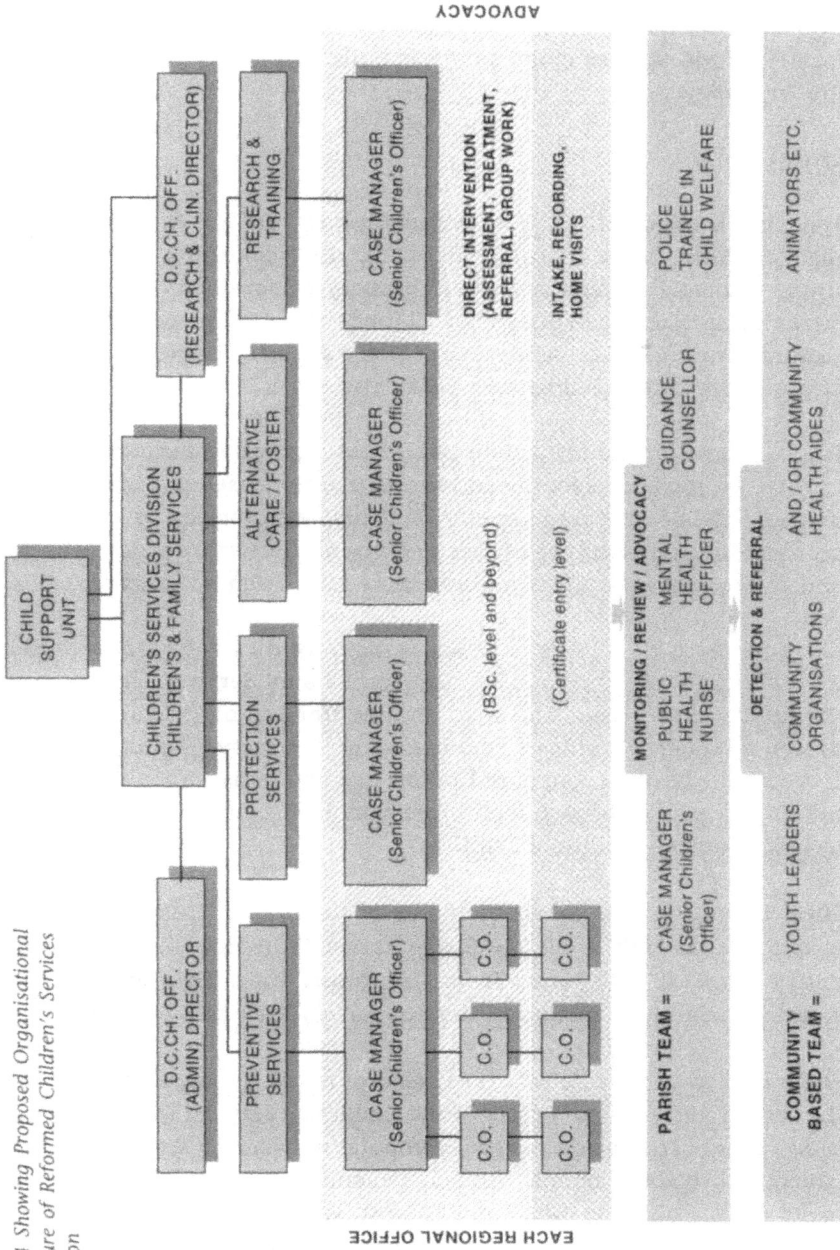

Fig.1.4 Showing Proposed Organisational Structure of Reformed Children's Services Division

ADVOCACY

EACH REGIONAL OFFICE

CHILD SUPPORT UNIT

D.C.CH.OFF. (ADMIN) DIRECTOR

CHILDREN'S SERVICES DIVISION
CHILDREN'S & FAMILY SERVICES

D.C.CH.OFF. (RESEARCH & CLIN. DIRECTOR)

PREVENTIVE SERVICES

PROTECTION SERVICES

ALTERNATIVE CARE / FOSTER

RESEARCH & TRAINING

CASE MANAGER (Senior Children's Officer)

C.O.

(BSc. level and beyond)

(Certificate entry level)

DIRECT INTERVENTION (ASSESSMENT, TREATMENT, REFERRAL, GROUP WORK)

INTAKE, RECORDING, HOME VISITS

MONITORING / REVIEW / ADVOCACY

PARISH TEAM =
CASE MANAGER (Senior Children's Officer)
PUBLIC HEALTH NURSE
MENTAL HEALTH OFFICER
GUIDANCE COUNSELLOR
POLICE TRAINED IN CHILD WELFARE

DETECTION & REFERRAL

COMMUNITY BASED TEAM =
YOUTH LEADERS
COMMUNITY ORGANISATIONS
AND / OR COMMUNITY HEALTH AIDES
ANIMATORS ETC.

* C.O. - Children's Officer
* D.C.CH. - Deputy Chief Children's Officer

in this chapter for the creation of a strong research, evaluation, and training unit within the service itself which would be constantly responsive to the findings and the needs of the practitioners who work directly with the children. This will require major programmatic and policy changes, which include the following.

Structural Inputs

- There is a need to *restructure the present Children's Services Division* through the establishment of a post higher than chief children's officer for a strong technical professional whose primary responsibility would be for public child welfare. This would balance the strong medical/health welfare focus which presently exists in the Ministry of Health, possibly at the expense of the children's welfare sector.

- There is need for the institution of *efficient management practices* in the service, to include clear performance criteria based on operational policies set out in a clear operational policy statement of child care practice, to create improved levels of efficiency in social service delivery, and to reorient the system towards more child-friendly practices.

- There needs to be *ongoing in service training* for all levels of staff within the Children's Services Division, the Correctional Services Division and the Child Support Unit. This must include training of institutional staff as well as children's officers who must have a structured programme of continuing education, organized on an ongoing basis through in-service training as well as through their professional association, to update their technical and professional skills.

- There is need to reorient the mandate of the present children's agency to *focus on the child within the family*, rather than view the child as an entity separate and apart from the family unit. This suggests the establishment of an integrated service for children and families.

- There is need to provide *efficient systems of record keeping* throughout all the central and regional offices of the Children's Services Division. There is also a need to develop relevant computer networking systems through community bulletin boards, linking regional offices and linking allied social service agencies (the Family Court, Correctional Services, CVSS), as well as regional training and research institutions such as the University of the West Indies, the Caribbean Child Development Centre, and the University of Technology. These inputs must be put in place in order to standardize levels of service delivery, and content, which should interface with the National Children's Policy.

Research

Research must be made an integral aspect of the functioning of all agencies providing services for children. It must be used as a means of keeping track of the children in care, as well as a means of pointing to advocacy, programme planning and policy development (see Figure 1.4).

- The system of mass institutionalization as the primary means of meeting the needs of children needing alternate care should at least be reexamined and reevaluated to determine its effectiveness based on the cost, the quality of services delivered, and the extent to which the needs of the children are met. Research must also be done to keep tabs on children in institutions in terms of tracking their disposition and in terms of meeting their total needs.

- It is suggested that pilot projects be instituted and ongoing research projects done to compare the effectiveness of using alternative forms of care, such as group homes, to treat the most difficult cases of children who are not suited for home based care, for example foster care.

Programme Inputs

- The role of the present children's agencies should shift from one of providing custodial care only, to one providing preventive as well as therapeutic services and referrals.

- The role of sponsorship programmes, adoption services and foster care services must be upgraded and strengthened and made more efficient to provide effective alternatives to the institutionalization of children.
- The role of the family must be given preeminence and it must be assumed that even the worst possible families can be rehabilitated and helped to take care of their children.

- Demonstration projects involving the use of group homes or large foster homes with specially trained parents could be considered on a phased basis to replace some of the larger and most ineffective institutions.

- It is recommended that intensive assessment procedures be conducted for all children presently in institutions, with the object of reducing the number of children who must remain in them. Placement disposition meetings must be adopted to ensure that only those children who have no other options remain in the institutions. Treatment plans must be instituted as part of agency practices. Families should be advised as to agency schedules relating to the terms of treatment, and projected dates for the return of their children where this is indicated and appropriate.

- It is recommended that an NGO based coordinating council for children and families with a structure like the Juvenile Advisory Board be put in place, possibly with the partnership of the private sector, administrators of children's institutions and existing NGO groups who already have children's institutions as their mandate, such as The Jamaica Foundation for Children and The Children's Lobby. It is important to note that this body need not be a new one, but could exist as a strengthened form of old structures.

- A system of community based follow up care supervised by trained officers of the Children's Services Division should be implemented, involving family counselling and extensive ongoing parenting education programmes. Follow up care should be put in place for those families whose children are at risk for placement, and those families whose children have been returned for home treatment.

- If institutions are to be used effectively, they should be rationalized to provide specialized care for children with different needs. Thus, adequate resources could be put into each institution to provide maximum care. It is recommended that if some of these institutions are closed, others could be more efficiently used for specialized services such as behaviour modification for uncontrollable youth, or for facilitating skills training of those children who may not be interested in pursuing academic subjects. At these centralized facilities, therefore, they could receive remedial education as well as training in marketable skills such as hair braiding, carpentry, agriculture, animal husbandry, and catering.

- Each institution needs to have access to the services of a clinical social worker and/or child psychologist at least once per month. This would provide assessment services as well as training and monitoring of individual and group treatment programmes run by institutional staff and/or local or regional staffers for those children who have emotional and behavioural problems and need ongoing treatment.

NOTES

1. Quoted in Kadushin (1967).
2. Children who are "home on trial" have been returned home after or during institutionalization for a specified period to evaluate and facilitate the adjustment of the child to the family, and vice versa.
3. Children who are "home on supervision" have been returned home, at the decision of a judge, with the order that they be supervised at home by a children's officer.
4. Child Month is celebrated in Jamaica in May, when children's agencies in the society at large are asked to focus on children's issues.
5. The Mico Counselling Centre offers skills training, personal development and services for the 11- to 18-year age group, but is largely underutilized by the Children's Services Division, due to the fact that the agency lacks a budget for specialized therapeutic services for its needy children.

RESOURCE MATERIAL

Books and Documents

Barnes, G. 1984. *Working with Families.* London: MacMillan Press.

Clough, R. 1982. *Residential Social Work.* London: MacMillan Press.

Crawford-Brown, C. 1987. *An Analysis of the Jamaican Child Welfare System*, Occasional Paper Series No. 1. Mona: Department of Sociology, University of the West Indies.

Family Services Committee Report. 1956. "The content of family social work", *Journal of Social Case-work*, July. New York: Family Service Association of America.

Friel, L. 1973. *Components of a System of Child Welfare.* Boston: Committee on Children and Youth.

Fox-Harding, L. 1996. *The Family, the State, and Social Policy.* London: MacMillan Press.

Herbert, M. 1988. *Working with Children and their Families.* London: British Psychological Society.

Marsh, O.D. 1994. *Children in Especially Difficult Circumstances, Policy Development and Review of Legislation in Jamaica.* Kingston, Jamaica: Child Support Unit, Ministry of Local Goverment, Youth and Sports/UNICEF.

Reistroff, M. 1974. *What you Always Wanted to Discuss About Foster-Care but did not Have the Time or Chance to Ask.* New York: Child Welfare League of America.

Sayle, E. 1994. *The First Fifty Years.* Kingston, Jamaica: Kingston Publishers.

Schulman, E. 1978. *Intervention in Human Services.* St. Louis: C.V. Mosby.

Smith, C. 1988. *Adoption and Fostering.* London: MacMillan Press.

Referral Sources and Agency Contacts

1. **Programme and Policy Development for Children**

   The Child Support Unit
   Central Projects Unit
   Ministry of Health
   11a Dumfries Road
   Kingston 5

   UNICEF
   Knutsford Boulevard
   Kingston 5

   The Children's Lobby
   c/o Department of Sociology and
   Social Work

University of the West Indies
Mona, Kingston 7

Caribbean Child Development Centre
School of Continuing Studies
c/o University of the West Indies
Mona, Kingston 7

Jamaica Association of Social Workers
c/o Medical Social Work Department
University Hospital of the West Indies
Kingston 7

2. **Children's Services Division
(Child Protection Services)**

The Ministry of Health
Children's Services Division
10A Chelsea Avenue
Kingston 10

3. **Regional Offices, Children's
Services Division**

South-East Area (Head Office)
10A Chelsea Avenue
Kingston 10

South-Central Area
9 North Race Course
Mandeville P O
Manchester

South-West Area
Santa Cruz P O
St. Elizabeth
North-East Area
Highgate P O
St Mary

4. **Children's Services Division,
Children's Homes
(Corporate Area)**

Alpha Boys' School
26 South Camp Road
Kingston 4

Best Care Lodge
9 Trevennion Road
Kingston 5

Maxfield Park Children's Home
89 Maxfield Avenue
Kingston 13

Musgrave Girls' Home
24 Lady Musgrave Road
Kingston 5

National Children's Home
Hope Gardens
Kingston 6

Rubella Unit
57 Mannings Hill Road
Kingston 8

St Andrew Hostel
16 Ellesmere Road
Kingston 10

The Nest
57 Mannings Hill Road
Kingston 8

5. **Children's Homes (Rural Areas)**

Hanbury Children's Home
Shooters Hill
Mandeville P O
Manchester

Blossom Gardens Child Care Centre
8 Coke Avenue
Morant Bay P O
St Thomas

Lyndale Children's Home
Highgate P O
St Mary

St John's Bosco
Hadfield P O
Mandeville
Manchester

St Monica's Home
Chapelton P O
Clarendon

Swift Purcell
Highgate P O
St Mary

Windsor Lodge
Williamsfield P.O.
Mandeville
Manchester

Windsor Girl's Home
St Ann's Bay P O
St Ann

2

Children
In Need of
Protection

INTRODUCTION

Throughout the 1990s, the Child Guidance Clinic reported that increasing numbers of adults in Jamaica did not seem to be able to cope with the responsibility of being effective parents, and resorted to abusing and neglecting their children. In 1984 the number of reported abused and neglected children was 400. In the two year period between 1993 and 1995 the number of reported cases was 3,500 (Child Guidance Clinic 1995). The increased numbers may have been due to increased reporting; however, the fact is that physical punishment was, and still is, seen as an important and necessary aspect of child rearing practice. The notion of children's rights, particularly the right not to be physically and/or sexually abused, does not appear to be in the forefront of public consciousness in the Jamaican society. The following discussion highlights the problems of children needing protection. These children need protection, not only from physical punishment by way of traditional abusers in their homes, but also from institutional and societal abuse, by way of the transportation system, for example, which has proved to be one of the most abusive social services inflicted on the young and old throughout the 1980s and 1990s. Inadequate parenting, the effects of migration, and the scourge of AIDS are just some of the problems highlighted in this chapter. Suggestions are offered as to what needs to be done at the macro level, through changing policies and systems, at the mezzo level through community based participation, and at the micro or interpersonal level.

CHILD ABUSE AND NEGLECT IN JAMAICA

Abuse of Young Children

(The following commentary was written as a response to the death of a two year old infant in one rural community in Jamaica at the hands of her father after she wet her bed. She died as a result of injuries she sustained when she was thrown to the floor.)

Children are singled out by the laws and by the cultural practices of most civilized societies in the world for special attention because it is assumed that they are not intellectually, physically, or emotionally capable of protecting themselves or their own interests. Child welfare systems are therefore developed by most societies as safety nets for children when there is breakdown in the family or when there are disasters. These systems should therefore act to protect the rights and best interests of the child at all times.

Practitioners who work in the agencies that make up a child welfare system should be advocates for their clients, constantly working to ensure that they are doing their best to promote and protect the welfare of the children they serve. Many who work or have worked with Jamaican children and families in the area of social service delivery have known for a long time that our children, particularly the ones who are most disadvantaged, are getting a raw deal. They are not being treated fairly. The issue that best depicts what is wrong with the delivery of child welfare services in this nation is that of the abuse and neglect of our children in all its forms. In order for any agency (NGO or government) to really deal with child abuse meaningfully, there must be a realization that the agency that is given the authority and responsibility, by law, to protect the interest of the abused child must be given the necessary human and material resources to do the job. This means that it needs well trained staff and adequate transportation facilities to support the extensive travelling that is routinely required to get the job done. It also means that the agency must have the credibility to convince the government (through its systems of evaluation, empirically based programme development, and systems of accountability based on client focused treatment methods) that it is an entity worth putting money into, in terms of its ability to manage, and prevent, cases of abuse and neglect of children.

The fact is that we are on the brink of the twenty-first century. Almost every other sector of our society is receiving some attention from the policy makers and planners who are attempting to find solutions to our social problems, yet many of us in the social services become defensive when challenged and prefer to complain about government not paying attention to us. In a society like ours where there are scarce resources, it is those who make themselves heard who get the attention.

The Responsibility of Children's Service Agencies

We say we care about the children we serve, but if we are not part of the solution, we are part of the problem! How many more of our children must die in this so called "caring" society of ours before we, the practitioners who work in the system, demand a better managed, more efficient child welfare system, which functions in the best interest of our children? The death of each child from an abusive parent must be seen as an indictment on each and every professional social worker whose mandate it is to protect our children.

Prevention Programmes: Could We Have Saved Lives?

The physical and sexual abuse of Jamaican children from infancy to adolescence continues to shock and frustrate the caring adult population of this country. The fact is, however, that these incidents, sensational as they are, have been shocking these same caring adults for many years. The problem of child abuse, therefore, does not go away because of expressions of righteous indignation. In fact these problems will never go away completely in any society but they can be considerably lessened if the society is organized to deal with them through carefully designed policies and programmes of prevention and intervention instituted by the agencies that come into contact with abused children on a regular basis. These include hospitals, schools and other governmental as well as non-governmental organizations. However, one gets the impression that the agencies responsible for managing the problems of child abuse in Jamaica are (i) not aware of the nature of the problems of child abuse, and/or (ii) do not have the necessary resources to tackle the problems efficiently and effectively in the areas of prevention and management. There is need for the restructuring of the government children's service agency to reflect an emphasis on the twin issues of *prevention*, which would include public education and parenting, and *protection*, whereby there would be more emphasis on individual and group intervention.

Effective Models Exist

Effective methods for dealing with the prevention and management of child abuse at a macro policy level, as well as the micro level of direct intervention with families and children, are well established in the developing and developed world, and therefore the knowledge base is widely accessible. Some models rely heavily on the use of a school based child study team for early detection and assessment. Other models focus strictly on child protection, using the child welfare system. For years Jamaican social workers, medical practitioners, nurses and teachers have been attending and participating in seminars, workshops and conferences on the problems of child abuse and neglect in Jamaica. As Child Month[1] passes each year, and the years go by, many speeches and papers have been presented on what needs to be done in terms of policy and intervention. The tireless work of researchers and pioneers such as Dr Denise Eldemire and Dr Pauline Milbourne is well documented, so we all know what must be done, yet much remains undone. We do not have an integrated and comprehensive approach nationally for dealing rationally with the problems of physical and sexual abuse of our children. Though workshops have been held and strategies written, effective large scale prevention and treatment programmes for the abused and for the abusers remain unrealized for most abused as well as for abusive families. This is partly due to the fact that the problem is by its nature a complex one which needs a multifaceted approach targeted at different levels of this social and cultural life.

Cultural Tolerance and Complacency

Other societies that have tackled this problem have found that effective approaches must be undergirded by government action in terms of concrete plans and policies, as the effective management of child abuse impacts on many

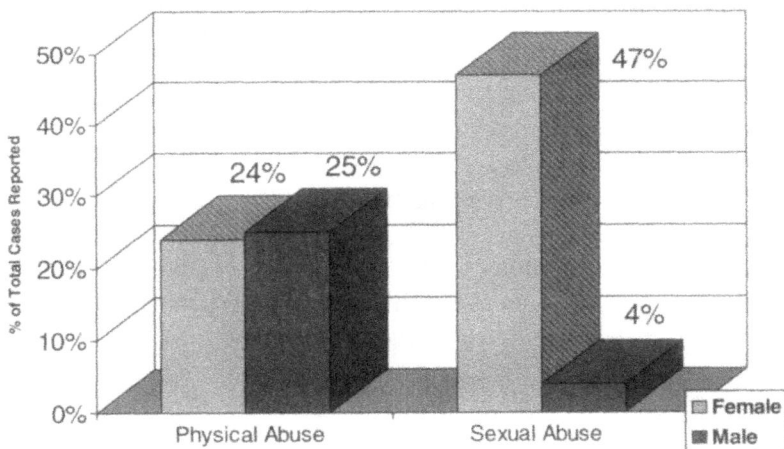

Fig. 2.1 Showing Abuse and Neglect Cases by Type and Sex 1988-89 Child Abuse Data

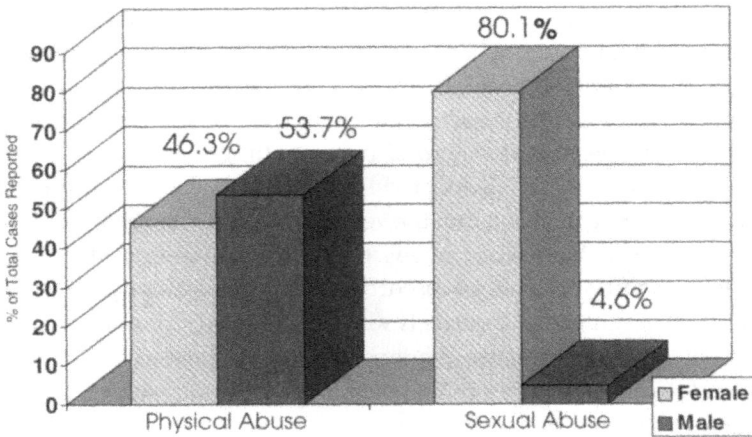

Fig. 2.2: Showing Abuse and Neglect Cases by Type and Sex 1991-92 Child Abuse Data

important aspects of our social and cultural life. For example, child prostitution (male and female) in the urban areas of Jamaica is fostered by widespread cultural complacency and attitudes that allow the sexual abuse of our very young children to go unchallenged. The fact that reported cases of sexual and physical abuse remain at unacceptable levels is cause for concern, with the incidence of reported cases of physical abuse being marginally higher in males (25 percent) than in females (24 percent), and the reported cases of sexual abuse being disproportionately higher in girls (see Figures 2.1 and 2.2).

Sexual molestation of school girls within the context of the overcrowded transportation system is another aspect of the societal attitude that allows sexual abuse to go unchallenged. What can be done to address these issues in a firm definitive way once and for all? The following sections summarize the major policy recommendations made over the years.

Strategies for Programme Development

The development of programmes must be standardized across the country and must be structured through the use of an interdisciplinary protocol. This protocol should include the basic components identified below.

Child Abuse Policies and Protocol

Child welfare authorities must be prevailed upon to develop and put in place a broad and comprehensive, written policy on children and families, which must be broken down to include policies for the different agencies working with children. The Children's Services Division, for example, must have operational policies that set out clear procedures and a particular protocol to deal with child abuse and neglect across the different social service and law enforcement agencies. The content of this policy must be disseminated to the broadest range of social work practitioners who work with children and their families. These practitioners should include community development practitioners in the Social Development Commission, correctional officers in the Ministry of National Security and Justice, children's officers in the Ministry of Health, as well as social workers in the NGO community. This is a basic prerequisite for any modern government agency dealing with the global, social and economic realities of the twenty-first century.

Family Treatment: Basic Prerequisite for Management

If we are to implement an effective child abuse management programme, such a policy must make provision for the ongoing assessment and treatment of the abusive family as well as the victim. The abuser must be held accountable in any child abuse management scenario, where abusers must go to counselling or else they go to jail. At present the treatment of the abuser is not written into the programming and policies of the existing Jamaican child welfare system. This means that we are not getting to the root of the problem. We only disrupt the life of the child, leaving the abuser to victimize other children.

Interagency Collaboration: Parish Committees

Implicit in all aspects of the child abuse management procedure must be the notion of interagency collaboration and team work. A multidisciplinary approach should therefore be adopted to undergird any management strategy to address this problem effectively. This would involve the use of child abuse committees, which must be instituted and strengthened at the parish and community levels. Such committees should involve professionals or representatives of professionals who work with these children and their families on a regular basis. These committees were originally proposed several years ago by Dr Pauline Milbourne of the Child Guidance Clinic in the Ministry of Health (Milbourne 1995). There is need for these committees to be strengthened where they already exist, and instituted in those parishes where they are absent. These committees should be institutionalized as an important aspect of the operation of a comprehensive child protection system. They should operate to support the existing government agencies in the area of monitoring follow up activities, and as a mechanism for the referral of cases from the community, via community based representatives on the parish committees. Parish committees could consist of a medical or a mental health officer, a professional social worker, a police officer, a teacher and/or guidance counsellor. Parishes could also add resource persons in the areas of child psychology, law and other areas, depending on the resources of the community.

Operational Guidelines

The writing and dissemination of operational guidelines for the child protective services must be made a priority of the child welfare system. These guidelines must include the development of a comprehensive child abuse manual.

Management and Intervention: Child Abuse Manuals

The parish teams mentioned above could be guided in their activities by a management and intervention programme. This should be outlined in a series of child abuse manuals, highlighting various aspects of the management of the problem. These manuals should specify who does what, as well as how to proceed, in a step by step fashion. These manuals could be written by a technocrat initially, but must have suggestions and feedback from social workers as well as health professionals with various children services agencies and health service agencies. They should be circulated to all practitioners, who would then have a standardized methodology for intervention. Manuals should be upgraded at least every five years. This would help to address the problem of the fragmented way in which these cases are currently managed.

Comprehensive Training in Basic Detection and Assessment Techniques

The comprehensive training of all agency staff, inclusive of hospitals, particularly medical social work departments where they exist, or social work agencies, schools and relevant members of the police force, on the use of child abuse manuals, as well as training in the use of established child welfare protocol suited to the Jamaican environment must be made an urgent priority. Sensitization of all staff to the nature of the problem must be of the utmost importance at all levels of intervention, across different agencies. This would prevent, for example, the multiplicity of interviews of child abuse victims by different agencies and would streamline the process of data collection so vitally needed for further planning. It would also deal with the practice of child abuse victims being paraded by the media to the public, which can be very detrimental to the child.

Specialist Training

A specialist training course in child and family welfare should be introduced at the tertiary graduate level for social workers and social work administrators. Modules of such a course could be offered as part of continuing education programmes, so that the skills of practitioners can be upgraded on an ongoing basis. With the institution of specialist protection and prevention services there will be need for creative and well designed child abuse prevention and child protection in service training programmes for staff of the Children's Services Division and the Department of Correctional Services, as well as the Family Court. Coordinated in service training must be established within these agencies as the first step towards offering high quality and integrated services to children, families and communities.

Public Education Programmes/Role of the Media

Parent education programmes must also be an essential component of an integrated system of service delivery. The absence of strong parent education and public education programmes is currently producing a situation where abused children remain one of the most vulnerable, unsupported, and helpless groups of disadvantaged children in the country. The media in Jamaica in the 1990s should see this need as a challenge, and should not allow this situation to continue. There is need for media intervention and public education at different levels, in the form of policy analyses, dissemination of data and general information, in a format that the average parent or child can understand. The incidents of school age children allowing strangers to inject them, which were reported to occur in rural Jamaica in 1997, is a testament to our inability to educate our young children about the very basics of personal safety. The media has an important role in providing consistent and ongoing public information on all matters and issues affecting children. It should not be a one-month affair, nor should it be a matter of sensationalism attached to a particular incident. Our children and our parents deserve more sustained attention and intelligent analysis from the media on an ongoing basis.

Mandatory Reporting

Necessary legislation should be enacted to make it mandatory for medical practitioners, teachers and social workers to report cases of abuse to the relevant authorities. Several agencies and individuals such as the CVSS, and retired social policy practitioners like Gloria Cumper (now deceased), and social workers such as Mrs Inez Morrison have worked tirelessly in the area for many years and have identified the aspects of the law that need to be addressed. The present legislation results in situations where cases of child abuse in the middle class are handled differently from those that occur in the lower economic groupings. Consequently, perpetrators are not held responsible or accountable and therefore many do not receive treatment, punishment or any other form of intervention.

Accountability for Abusers

Abusers must be held accountable to go to counselling or go to jail. There needs to be a focus on establishing treatment and/or punishment regimens for perpetrators as well as using the threat of punishment to enforce treatment. Many abusive families can be helped and children do not always have to be "yanked" unceremoniously out of their schools and homes and placed in institutions as a method of treatment and intervention, while the abusers remain in the comfort of their own homes, untreated, unpunished and not required to be accountable for their actions.

The Management of Child Abuse in the School System

The assessment and management of child abuse in the school system, as well as the management of child abuse cases in child care institutions, must also be addressed. This is a wide open area in the Jamaican society which has a variety of cultural underpinnings and needs urgent and careful attention in terms of policy and action, through such organizations as the Jamaica Teachers Association (JTA), and the Association of Child Care Employees (ACCE). Specialized training for teachers and child care workers, and the designation of an appropriately trained individual in each institution to handle all child abuse cases are important first steps.

Monitoring and Evaluation for Quality Assurance

Creative monitoring and evaluation of the quality of service delivery for different agencies working with abused children, such as schools, as well as NGO and government children's services agencies, is vital for bringing about improvements in service. This monitoring should be done in terms of agency functioning as well as client satisfaction, through the use of the long proposed interdisciplinary parish committees. We need to know on an ongoing basis how effective our protective services are in treating the children and their families who are referred to them. Simple quality assurance systems instituted within the child welfare system would help to answer these questions, and could eventually improve other areas of service delivery to children and families.

Development of a National Database

This suggests the need for a national database which, among other things, would include information on the incidence of child abuse. Some of this information would allow for updating and mapping of long term trends and could therefore inform future policy. Databases in these areas already exist in social policy data banks at some tertiary institutions and planning agencies. These large databases must be "harvested", however, to produce the specific information needed for the child welfare system. Once a child welfare database is established, it should have the following characteristics:

- Information must be collected annually, and should be translated into a readable format for practitioners of NGO or other agencies to ensure dissemination of data across a range of agencies working with and for children at different levels (for example, advocacy and children's rights groups as well as NGOs and government agencies working directly with children and their families).
- The database should be able to produce concise information on the status of abused children, as well as on related areas, for example, the status of children without homes, children out of school, children who are working, and how these correlate with the figures on child abuse. This information presently exists but it must be collected and collated in a systematic and regular manner to ensure credibility.
- Such a database must be able to tell us where our abused children are coming from in terms of geographical area and socioeconomic status. We need to know the gender of children being abused and what factors are causing them to be abused. Small sporadic studies have been done in the past, but these need to be more consistent and must be national studies to have meaning and relevance for planning.

This is the kind of detailed research data that needs to emanate from the main children's agency with the assistance of the Child Support Unit. Attempts by the NGO sector to do this kind of research have met with little support from the few funding agencies willing to invest in research, while corporate donors often do not see research of this nature as important to enhance their image. They prefer high profile Christmas treats, for example. The government must therefore take an interest in this kind of research, and provide the resources to do this kind of work, as scarce international funding is receding. Assistance to NGOs to provide this kind of data is essential if we are to really move forward to provide more efficient children's services in the future.

Strategies for Policy Formulation on Child Abuse

Over the past ten years government policies from our major political parties in relation to child abuse, like other aspects of child welfare, have consisted of "surface-level" statements which are seemingly based on good intentions towards children. Many of these statements, however, have not been backed by action at the highest levels, nor have they received real support in terms of the appropriate allocation of resources. These statements are usually trotted out for budget debates, and other symbolic occasions such as Child Month and Christmas time, but the necessary political will and resources to do something meaningful (in terms of dealing with the fundamental problems of ineffectiveness and inefficiency in the operation of the child welfare system) remains absent. The verbal statements and platitudes regarding the government's commitment to children will not be able to get us through to the twenty-first century.

Viewing children's affairs as everybody's portfolio, and thinking of a policy for child abuse as nice sounding platitudes on their behalf will not do, as we move forward into the future. We have a tendency to focus on the symptoms of our problems, such as crime and violence, street children, AIDS and child prostitution. Such problems are not going to go away, and will in fact become more severe as the new century approaches. In terms of providing a dynamic and ongoing programme of policy development, the child welfare system in Jamaica has yet to effectively address the social problems of the twentieth century in this way. The following represent practical suggestions for the ways in which policy development and formulation can be effectively implemented.

Open Parliamentary Hearings

Open, regularly scheduled parliamentary hearings on child abuse and other child protection issues could be used as an effective strategy for the development of policy guidelines which will allow social service agencies and advocacy groups to report to small parliamentary meetings on those aspects of policy they would like to see adopted. Researchers should also be given a chance to report to these hearings to give their informed opinions. This could be an important first step to developing operational guidelines that would be applicable nationally.

Development of a Resource Facility

A resource facility to house the national database and all other information concerning Jamaican child welfare written and produced over the years is also essential. At present, information on Jamaican child welfare issues is scattered across various agencies in the government and the NGO sector and is almost inaccessible. Our children's future demands that we have such a facility located in a governmant agency or in a tertiary institution, where research information as well as other resource material (such as video and audio tapes, pamphlets, brochures, manuals and other available intervention tools) are readily available, preferably in a summative form, online, for the use of researchers, practitioners, planners, students, and others who may need this information.

These are just some of the many aspects of the management of the physical and sexual abuse of children in Jamaica that must be addressed in a comprehensive and intelligent manner. We already have agencies that have been working in this area, and a great deal of work has already been done. The piecemeal, individualistic way in which we have addressed this problem as individuals and agencies, however, cannot continue. We have the information and the expertise to tackle the problem but there is need for:

(a)   Basic resources to be committed to this area for a specified period;
(b)   The implementation by government of these policies and the supportive programmes to address the issue of child abuse and neglect in a focused, systematic and sustainable manner;
(c)   The collection and collation of all the available information through these established agencies of government.

Once the data have been analyzed, the information must be disseminated nationally, so that every practitioner at the community level, urban or rural, knows what to do and how to deal with the problem in terms of a prevention/ intervention protocol, as well as its management.

Electronic Community Bulletin Board

One way of achieving the latter goal with a minimum of expenditure is through the establishment of a simple community bulletin board system where existing information on child welfare in Jamaica can be shared and new information from research at tertiary institutions and beyond can be accessed by service providers and practitioners in the field, via the Internet. We cannot continue to hope that "something will be done soon", as one television news commentator suggested in 1994. Our children are crying out, males and females, adolescents, preschoolers and infants. They cannot be expected to endure much more. There seems to be some difficulty in seeing the connection between the delay in implementing policies and programmes for abused children, and the presence of deviant, violent and criminal adults in our society. The time for action is now. The children have waited long enough. Tomorrow will be too late!

CHILDREN IN VIOLENT COMMUNITIES

A number of violent actions against children, which have been reported in the news media over the 1980s and 1990s, have riveted themselves on the consciousness of many of us as individuals and as a society. These images included the agonizing pictures of the lifeless bodies of little ones killed in numerous vehicular accidents in the last decade. Other images include those of a sobbing seven year old boy cradled in the arms of his adult brother, after the gun slaying of his mother in Franklin Town. There was a picture of a five year old girl from an east rural parish, whose left arm was chopped off by a strange man who tried to get her to go off with him. When she refused, one newspaper report stated, the adult assailant used a machete to sever her left arm completely, just below the elbow. These types of incidents were repeated many times over throughout the 1980s and into the 1990s. Even as this manuscript goes to press the horror stories continue. These reports have sent feelings of horror, shock, a sense of shame, and, unfortunately, a feeling of paralysis among many of us, because we do not know what to do. During 1996 and 1997 several children were shot dead or injured, intentionally and accidentally, by groups of marauding gunmen, some as young as fifteen years old. These incidents fuel in some of us a sense of urgency about the current status of children in Jamaica, in terms of their physical safety, and in terms of their psychological well being.

Children and Violence: Solutions

The problem of violence against children, like the problems of violence in Jamaican society generally, is quite complex, and it is therefore important that policy makers and planners resist the temptation to adopt a blinkered perspective on solutions that dictate only one possible path, to the exclusion of all others. The problems that cause violence in Jamaica are multifactorial and multilevelled. Solutions therefore have to be similarly structured, and must operate at the macro policy level, making use of empirical research that is grounded in the reality of the children's experiences. For example, findings from a preliminary pilot study of children under 12 years in one inner city community speak to the need for what could be referred to as the *strengthening of their coping abilities* through spiritual guidance and the need for significant others to talk to about their fears (Dean 1997). In order to really help these children in a meaningful way, therefore, solutions cannot be focused on any one model or any one mode of intervention, and must not only look at the macro level, but must also work simultaneously at the mezzo level within the community, helping each community to find its own solutions, as this is the context within which the violence takes place. At the same time the children and their families have very urgent and burning needs at the micro level for support and assistance, materially as well as emotionally. These needs must also be addressed by service providers with some technical competence (albeit within the limits of our human resources), if we are to prevent further violence in the future.

Play Spaces for Children as a Violence Prevention Strategy

Community parks with play spaces for children can be used as a means of providing positive alternative agencies of socialization and establishing safe havens and respite for children and families needing a 'breather' from some of the violence, particularly in and around some of our urban communities. Urban dwellers in Jamaica are starved for green spaces and play spaces for children, and urban planners must be sensitized to the need to include such spaces in our suburban as well as our inner city communities. It is worthy of note that very few of our international and local family restaurants have seen fit to erect play spaces for children in their places of business, a very popular strategy instituted in most other countries. The Children's Lobby has been encouraging the international franchises to establish these play areas in the urban areas for some time. In the same way that french fries and hamburger patties are imported, one would assume that the components for play equipment could also be imported, with the play equipment at least having some sustainability in terms of providing much needed recreational play space for our nation's children.

From the above discussion it is apparent that we must harness the energies of the NGO and government sectors that provide services to children and families and coordinate their activities in such a way that they see themselves as working as a team towards a common goal. The Children's Service Agency must take a lead role in providing efficient and effective services to families but must understand the role and function of the NGO sector in supporting their efforts to provide comprehensive services, and must clearly see how their activities complement and interact with all the other child and family agencies in the social service network (see Figure 2.3).

Fig. 2.3 Referral Channels for Integrated Services (Children at Risk)

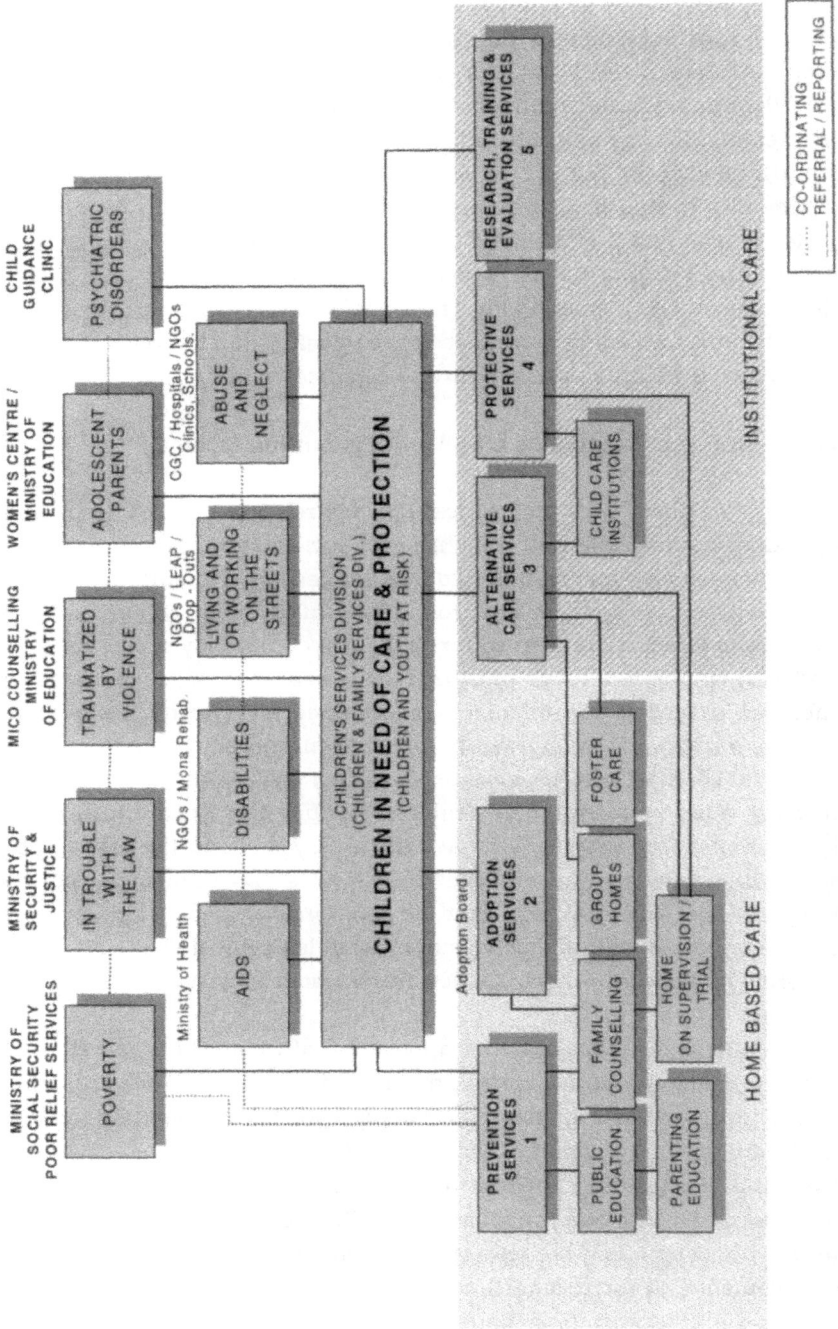

Another issue that needs to be addressed in looking at violence against children is the need to look at the societal factors that have transported us into what seems to be an unholy mess.

CHILDREN AND THE TRANSPORTATION SYSTEM

Children as Pedestrians

Whenever people are killed on our roads, particularly children, we hear pronouncements from the police about the need to abide by the traffic laws, and a few advertisements are trotted out by the information services, but the killings continue unabated. In the past four years (1992-1996), we are informed that four hundred children were killed on our roads. Many of these deaths could have been prevented. This suggests that we have to go beyond the approach of using low powered advertisements and sporadic public education to get people to obey the laws and rules of the road. When we look at the data, we realize that the children and adults being killed in traffic accidents are passengers and pedestrians, and the victims seem to be mainly adults and children of the working class.[2]

Children of the Middle Class: Cellular Phones and Safety

Middle class children and adults who go everywhere in cars are also at risk, however, because children continue to be driven around without being buckled in car seats, and are allowed to stand on front seats while their parents drive around at high speeds. Many of these parents use the ever popular cellular phone as they drive. The use of cellular phones while driving was recently described by one member of the National Safety Council as not a contributor to accidents on our roads. The reason given by this eminent person was based upon the fact that he possesses a cellular phone which he uses while driving and he was not a danger to others. According to this individual charged with the responsibility to assist in the development of policies to make our roads safer, there was therefore no need to look at this area of road safety. This is not good enough in a society where there is so much carnage on our roads.

Seat Belts and Bicycle Helmets

One must commend the initiative of the late Professor Sir John Golding and the work of the Road Safety Committee for pushing for legislation to enforce the wearing of seat belts, bike helmets, and the use of breathalyser tests. However, for the Jamaica of today, our efforts cannot stop here. These measures and messages do not address or reach the minds of the potential killer drivers, who proliferate in urban and rural Jamaica. These measures also do not help the pedestrian child whose mother sends him off to school clean and neat with his little lunch box, only to see him next in a morgue with the little lunch box still clutched in his hand. The Montpelier case in 1994 where five children were killed by a motor vehicle while they were waiting on a bus for school, was not one of parental neglect, and in this present traffic scenario it can happen again and again, as occurred in Walkerswood in November 1996 when three children were killed on their way to school. This occurred again and again throughout 1997. We must try to see to it that there is a reduction of such incidents. The following are some concrete recommendations for improving the situation.

Child Safety Initiatives

Distribution of Child Safety Material

Child safety material in the form of booklets and videotapes should be developed for our society and should be shown and distributed at PTA meetings, antenatal clinics, health centres, car licensing offices and revenue centres, to allow basic information to be disseminated about the special needs of children, and how to prevent and prepare children to be good pedestrians. Such material could deal with the prevention of accidents and the promotion of safety generally, and should focus specifically on children from infancy to adolescence. The importance of seat belts and bicycle helmets must be given priority, with the government considering subsidizing the cost of bicycle helmets for children in primary schools if they ride, or if their parents ride them to school on motorbikes or bicycles. Safety messages must be repeated by the media over and over again until our drivers and our citizenry get the message.

Billboards Portraying Child Victims

The killing of children on our roads should be the cornerstone of a national assault on the conscience and consciousness of the potential killer drivers. Future public education and prevention programmes should revolve around the children who have been victims of road accidents over the years. The use of pictures of these children on our billboards and also in the written and electronic media could be used as a deterrent to dangerous driving. (Of course, the permission of family members would have to be sought in such an endeavour.) If these billboards are located in close proximity to the communities from which the children originated, the source of funding could be community based.

The Community Response

Community action groups made up of grass roots community persons, including parents or families who have lost their children due to violence such as this, could be used to mobilize funds to keep the deaths of these children in the consciousness of our drivers. In this way, we will not forget how these children and others died. Mothers Against Drunk Drivers (MADD) has been a very effective advocacy group using similar strategies in other countries. Involvement in such a group could also be therapeutic for the parents and families who often have no source of counselling or other support, particularly in the rural areas. The community groups could use videotapes to involve survivors who may want to speak about their feelings and the impact of the death of their loved ones on their lives. These tapes could be used for treating the perpetrators, training social work practitioners, mediation counsellors, guidance counsellors, and others involved in direct intervention with the victims of this and other forms of violence. This training could be instituted as part of an ongoing violence prevention programme which could be administered by social work, psychology or allied programmes at tertiary institutions. In this way, practitioners at different levels could be trained systematically over time.

One community based group, Parents of Inner-City Kids (PICK) already exists in one inner city community in Kingston. The activities of this group should be strengthened and possibly replicated and used as a model in other areas. This group functions as a support group to mothers who have lost their children to violence and provides an essential service to parents and families traumatized by the violence that has engulfed sections of our urban landscape in recent years.

Law Enforcement

We must strengthen these community approaches with the relevant legal systems in place to enforce the laws, so that the irresponsible drivers cannot be allowed back on the streets within months, ready to kill another child, without counselling, without being forced to do community service and without being held accountable for their actions in one way or another.

Children as Passengers

There is a very urgent need for joint action by community based organizations such as the consumer groups, and the women's and children's organizations and associations, to challenge the government to do something concrete about the transportation system.

The present situation is untenable, and has been for years. The government of the day must be aware of the fact that the society does not accept the nightmare of the present transportation service. However, many of us have no choice. Children are one of the vulnerable groups in our society who suffer greatly under the present system. They are verbally abused, and some have been pushed off the buses on occasion, some crushed to death. We will always remember little Jeremy Small, who was pushed under the wheels of a bus in urban Jamaica in 1995. After his death we got school buses, but school buses without schedules, and buses without highly motivated, well trained staff meant little or no change in the way children were treated on the buses. Children continue to be exposed to violence and aggression on an ongoing basis, as well as lewd and sexually inappropriate behaviour. Children continue to be made to feel that they are a nuisance to the adult world. They have also become immune to the indiscipline and now demand loud music and fast driving as part of the basic components of transportation. We have created more than a monster. We have created a generation of children who accept abuse and mistreatment as part of their daily lives. Thus, we guarantee anarchy and mayhem for our future.

Looking Back

In comparing today's situation with the writer's own childhood experiences on the buses of the Jamaica Omnibus Service in the 1960s, there are sharp contrasts. On one occasion while travelling from downtown to Constant Spring, I remember standing on the bottom step of the "Jolly" bus, when a very portly female conductor, using a six-pence piece, knocked on an aluminum bar in the bus. It stopped immediately and the conductor said: "Hold on driver, a little girl is on the bottom step. The bus can't move off with her there like that. Come up little girl," she said. After I had moved up the steps into the bus, the conductor then signaled the bus to move off. At that point, I remember feeling special. I remember feeling protected, that I belonged to a society that cared. As a child I had a feeling that I was a valuable part of the society.

Today, the way we treat our children on the buses makes them feel that they need to get back at a society that treats them unkindly, harshly, and with disrespect. Thus are our violent adults born and nurtured while we continue to wring our hands and lament on our terrible and violent society. We stand and watch as if we are helpless to stop the anarchy into which we have thrown ourselves and our children.

Gender Issues in the Transportation Industry

At a policy seminar on the transportation system held by the Children's Lobby in 1995, questions were raised about the gender of the bus crew. The view was expressed that if the male conductors will not accept, and continue to resist, training, then the authorities should return to the practice of hiring female conductors, as happened during the time of the previous bus service. Those males who respond positively should be retained, it was felt, as good male conductors do exist. The general feeling from seminar participants was that the entry requirements for bus crews were too low. It was felt that drivers and conductors could not continue to be the rejects of the labour market.

Recommendations for Child Friendly Transportation

Recommendations from this seminar included a proposal that the Transportation Authority should sponsor regular public fora in which child advocacy groups, along with other organizations such as the consumer groups, and the Association of Women's Organizations in Jamaica (AWOJA), can jointly express their own proposals for improvements to the transportation system and possibly sign a massive petition to be taken to the Minister of Water and Transportation. We could then actively express our disgust with the present system, and demand urgent changes to allow our men, women and children to travel with dignity. Some of the proposals that must be part of any improved system include:

- A mandatory training school for conductors and drivers, which must include in its curriculum basic information on child and adult development, such as the developmental needs and rights of children, as well as the special needs of the elderly. Such training must be practical, using videotapes, drama, role play and other hands on exercises. The needs of the physically and mentally handicapped must also be included in this training programme. Graduation, on successful completion of this course, must be tied to the granting of the road license. If the bus crew applicant does not complete the training he or she should not be able to receive a permit or license to drive or to operate as a conductor on any form of public transportation carrying children: no training - no license. On graduation, each crew member could be presented with a certificate, badge or identification logo of their franchise, and a set of uniforms. If these exercises are given media attention and publicity, they could become attractive status boosters to the workers in the transportation system, who must be made to feel special and that they have an important part to play in the nation's development.

- On application for a job as part of a bus crew there should be some system of assessment which would indicate the suitability of the conductors or drivers for the job. This should include, if possible, some indication of the suitability of the candidate in terms of a psychological profile with regard to attitudes to children, the disabled, or the elderly, for example.
- There must be strict monitoring of the playing of music in the buses, particularly those with lyrics that are inappropriate for children. There should also be standards regarding decorations on buses and the general physical condition of buses. Children and adults should not be putting up umbrellas in the buses when it rains. We deserve better as a society and as a country.
- Any improved transportation system must be supported by a massive public education programme. The public is now so hardened, and so used to indiscipline, chaos and anarchy, and coarse interpersonal relationships, that there has to be a retraining of the public mind as well if we are to pull the transportation system out of the present state of chaos and degradation.

These are just some of the recommendations that could be put forward to a joint community based action committee for an improved and efficient transportation system.

CHILD PROSTITUTION IN JAMAICA

When the Children's Lobby was launched in Jamaica in 1986, the issue that was at the forefront of the public conscience at that time was the beginning of what seemed to be child prostitution in Jamaica. There were reports of children being exploited in nightclubs where they were "working" as dancers. At that time the news was sensational, and there was public outcry. The Children's Lobby at that time described the nature of prostitution as being rooted in economic factors. Many of the young girls, apart from dancing in nightclubs, were also approaching minibus drivers (or the local community "boops", now replaced by the "don") and were receiving support for school expenses in exchange for sexual favours. At that time the point was made that there was an urgent need to address the fundamental societal factors that were pushing children as young as eleven years into selling their as yet undeveloped bodies and destroying their future. It was suggested that the main "push" factors, which the social planners and policy makers in the areas of health, education, and social welfare needed to be aware of, were the effects of structural adjustment policies, and problems related to the migration of parents.

The Impact of Structural Adjustment Policies

Beginning in the 1980s, economic policies implemented by the government had the effect of biting hard into the pockets of low income families, resulting in basic school expenses becoming more unaffordable to more and more households. Social programmes to support families with children who were in genuine need were recommended to tackle this, as well as the overall problem of street children. Government officials at the time suggested that such a programme, using well trained welfare officers, would be impossible to implement, as our poverty pool was much too big and there was not enough money. Today we are reaping the seeds of the neglect of our children, as evidenced by the violence in our society. As a result we now have to find additional resources as a society to build more prisons and support these same children now turned adults during incarceration, as they pay their dues to society for the havoc they have wrought.

Problems of Parenting and Problems Relating to the Migration of Parents

Children in the upper, middle, and working classes continue to be victims of the migration experience, to the extent that one or both parents have been absent. Some children do not suffer undue hardships as a result, while others are relegated to the status of "barrel children", who are defined as children waiting to rejoin parents, who receive material gifts in barrels from parents who reside in the metropolitan capitals, but receive little emotional nurturing from these parents (Crawford-Brown and Rattray 1994). It has been determined that these children are at risk for a range of behavioural problems, including child prostitution, particularly in those instances where alternative parenting is inadequate.[3] It is important to note that the investigations of child prostitution at that time did not establish a cause/effect relationship between child prostitution and the "barrel children" phenomenon, but rather the investigators felt that a general problem of a lack of parental supervision was a contributory factor to the problem of child prostitution and child pornography, and within the context of inadequate parental supervision, some of these children could in fact fall into the category of "barrel children" as defined above.

BARREL CHILDREN

The term "barrel children" was coined by Jamaican social work practitioners within the last decade to describe a specific category of children waiting to rejoin parents who have migrated. These children receive material resources by way of goods packaged in barrels from the metropole but are emotionally deprived as a result of the absence of a parent. Children are affected by the migration experience in two major ways, either (i) the effect of migration on the family left behind in the Caribbean, or (ii) the effect of migration on the family in the host country when there is reunification.

It is important to understand the nature of the Caribbean migration experience in order for the practitioner to face the special challenges of working with the contemporary migrant Caribbean family.

Family Kinship Systems and the "Barrel Children" Syndrome

Thomas-Hope (1992) suggests that the kinship systems of the working class Caribbean family make migration of the mother possible, because there is a "reciprocal system of obligations". Children may therefore be left in the Caribbean with relatives, friends or neighbours. Family members, both of the household and wider family, traditionally help facilitate migration of a member through financial assistance or undertaking the responsibilities of the migrant. The child rearing responsibilities of the extended family are in turn compensated by the remittances or gifts, traditionally sent in corrugated cardboard barrels for the purposes of international shipping. Thus the evolution of the term "barrel children". Thomas-Hope (1992) suggests that the effect of a strong familial kinship network, as well as inheritance related land tenure patterns, allows mother or father to leave their young children for prolonged periods. These children are then expected to join them several years later. This migrating pattern is one of the most significant single factors affecting the Caribbean family. What are the effects of these factors on the family?

The Effects of Migration on the Family Left Behind in Jamaica

The effects of migration on families left behind in Jamaica revolve around issues of attachment, separation and loss, as experienced by the children left behind. Children left in Jamaica by their parents sometimes spend their entire lives struggling with feelings of rejection, abandonment and loss.

When family migration occurs in a serial manner, as occurs in Jamaica, with one family group migrating to the host country, followed by the others years later, there are other important implications that must be considered. The ritualised maintenance of contact during separation and the rituals surrounding reunification all have an important impact on the adaptation process.

It is estimated that when some Jamaican family members leave their country of origin, the period of separation between parent and child can vary between three and ten years. Some children are left as early as a few months old, others at very critical stages when separation is known to cause psychological damage (Bowlby 1953). Separation is difficult for both mother and child. For the child who is left at a very early age, the memory of the parent fades. For the child left at a later stage, there is fear, anger, resentment or a feeling of rejection. The effects of the separation process are later manifested through the absence of bonding between parent and child, the "strangeness" of the reunification and the antisocial tendencies acted out, which according to Winnicot (1956), represent a search on the one hand for something they have lost, and on the other hand for something they never had.

It is the view of some Caribbean writers (Crawford-Brown and Rattray 1994) that the problems experienced in the host country by Jamaican children at the levels of home, school and society are grief reactions. This is manifested on the part of the child in terms of withdrawal and anger, and on the part of the parent as guilt.

The Child's Behaviour in the Country of Origin

There are four theoretical factors that can be identified as affecting the child's behaviour in the country of origin (Lonner 1986). These include spatial, control, intra- and interpersonal factors, contributing to specific behavioural reactions in the child left in Jamaica. Spatial factors relate to the disorientation the child feels upon separation. Control factors relate to the notion that the migration process is usually outside of the child's control, and intra- and interpersonal factors relate to the difficulties experienced by the child in adjusting to new household members in his or her new family situation. These factors cause certain reactions in the child, which have an effect on his or her behaviour. These reactions present in a variety of ways and include deviant/acting out behaviour, withdrawal and depressive reactions, defensive behaviour, and runaway behaviour.

In a study on conduct-disordered behaviour among Jamaican male adolescents, it was determined that there was some association between the incidence of conduct disorder and the absence of mothers in the households of the adolescents studied. In that study, migration was found to be the most significant factor contributing to the absence of mothers in the delinquent group (Crawford-Brown 1993).

Recommendations for Working with Children of Migration

In order to deal with the problem of migration affecting children, parents should adhere to certain basic guidelines:

1. Parents should not remain separated from their children for prolonged periods. A child has a right to be parented by his or her biological parents. If this is not possible the following guidelines should apply.
2. Before parents separate from their children, they should make every effort to prepare the children for the separation. Children must be advised, in advance, of the nature of alternative parenting arrangements, and should be consulted on the available options.
3. If parents have to leave their children they should ensure that alternative child care is reliable and stable.
4. Parents should keep in touch with their children on a regular basis, through letters, phone calls, and visits. A parent who has separated from his or her child needs to develop creative ways to stay close to this child, for example by never forgetting birthdays. If a child has an examination the parent should try to call before or after that critical examination, or plan a vacation around the child's examination timetable so that he or she can be there.
5. There is need for an early warning and detection system in schools to pick up the root causes of the family problems associated with migration, as experienced by barrel children.

In addition there is need for comprehensive research to look at this problem nationally, to determine the numbers of children who are experiencing these problems within Jamaica and the Caribbean, so that proper plans and programmes can be developed for families and children in need.

The Absence of Early Warning Systems for Children at High Risk for Emotional and Psychological Problems

One gets the impression that over the years the Jamaican society has finally come to understand the need for an early detection system in the area of learning problems; hence the pressure on agencies like the Mico CARE Centre for early assessment of children with learning problems. There seems to be little understanding, however, that adolescents also need to be helped in terms of the detection of emotional and psychological problems. There is little evidence that there is a realization on the part of parents and educators that children need to be helped before there is breakdown in their families and before there is an erosion of parents' abilities to cope in the area of the management of emotional and behavioural problems. Social work practitioners started seeing, for example, the beginnings of childhood suicide during the 1980s, which has continued into the 1990s. The reality is that children are confronted at an early age with serious problems relating to early sexual activity (often sanctioned by parents), sexual abuse, as well as the problems associated with too many economic stresses and other family pressures. Without the necessary early warning and detection systems many children fall through the cracks and become the victims of child prostitution, an activity that many continue into adulthood.

Paradigm Shift in Child Welfare

The above discussion suggests that, in order to deal with the problem of child prostitution in a fundamental way, there is a need to shift our child welfare paradigm from one of custodial care and late intervention to one of prevention and early therapeutic intervention with families. Child prostitution, like most of the problems affecting children in Jamaica, is a symptom of family dysfunction. A shift towards the prevention of family breakdown can deal with the problem of child prostitution before it becomes intractable.

CHILDREN WITH AIDS

There has been much talk about the impact of the HIV virus and the consequent AIDS epidemic in Jamaican society. There have been regular reports on its incidence, its effect on families, and from time to time we get feedback on how communities are responding to this "new" disease. There has been little discussion, however, about the effect of HIV and AIDS on children in Jamaica, in terms of the specific policies and programmes that need to be put in place to assist children to cope, either with infection or with the impending death of one or both of their parents.

Incidence and Nature of the Disease

The latest figures, according to a UNICEF report, put the number of children with AIDS in Jamaica at 537 in 1995. The fact that so many children have become infected suggests that at least one aspect of the nature of the phenomenal spread of this disease in Jamaica is that the spread of the disease is due to heterosexual contact. This is similar to the pattern of affliction found in other developing countries in the region and elsewhere, such as Haiti and parts of Africa. The reality is that most of the children contracting the disease in Jamaica have become infected by their mothers who contract the disease from their infected male partners. To date the preliminary data that are available, from the limited research that has been done, do not point to direct infection, by children or adolescents contracting the disease from adult males such as occurs through child prostitution or other forms of sexual abuse. The fact that the children are contracting the disease from their mothers, however, raises specific challenges for those working with these children, as this fact points to the need to deal with this as a public health issue requiring widespread public education targeted intensively at the child bearing population. Though there has been much public education about HIV/AIDS targeted to the later adolescent and young adult child bearing population, there needs to be more advertising and public education directed at the older child rearing population regarding the devastating impact that HIV/AIDS has on the child who contracts the disease, in terms of the immediate effect on the health and subsequent mortality of the child.

Family Intervention

Some attention must be paid to parents infected with the virus, and those with full-blown AIDS, who need to be helped to cope with their impending death and all the implications of this, including separation from their children and significant others. Special programmes must also be put into place for children who need to be prepared for the death of one or both parents. These programmes could be set up through the existing hospice, or through the Family Centre (now the Centre for HIV, AIDS Research and Education Services, CHARES) of the University Hospital of the West Indies.

Tools for Working with Children with AIDS

One useful strategy that can be used for family intervention is the building of a symbolic bridge of contact between those who are going and those who will be left behind. This can be achieved through the use of life books, which are better known for their use in open adoptions (Frosh and Glaser 1988). Life books are books put together by a client, usually with the help of a social work professional. The life book is made up of pictures, souvenirs and other memorabilia that help the client who is being left behind to have a tangible memory of the person who is leaving. These books can be used with adoption cases as well as with clients who are dying. Some individuals have used video and audiotapes to permanently record their memories, which can be sources of comfort for those who are left behind, for years to come. Though these memories have a different impact on different people, individuals in this situation should be helped to understand their options so that they can make informed decisions about what they would like to leave behind. The life book makes use of the fact that the client who is going (for example a mother who is reluctantly giving up her child for adoption) may want to leave behind little "pieces of herself" so that her child will know that she loved her even though she had to give her up. In the case of a client who is dying from AIDS or some other chronic illness, the individuals involved usually have advance notice of the impending death. This does not make the acceptance of death any easier, and the person who is dying of AIDS has first to be helped through the different stages of dealing with his or her own death. The development of a life book can be an important part of the therapeutic process, particularly as it relates to the individual's relationship with his or her children.

Other tools that are useful in working with young children with AIDS are specially designed colouring books and other self-awareness work books, some of which are documented at the end of this chapter.

AIDS in the Classroom

At a breakfast seminar held by The Children's Lobby in 1995 to discuss policies relating to children with AIDS, a social worker from an agency working with families affected by AIDS pointed to the issue of the isolation that many children were faced with upon being diagnosed with the HIV virus. It was felt by participants at the conference that the question regarding the appropriate protocol for advising school officials was not clear. Some participants were concerned about whether schools should be informed at all, given confidentiality leaks evident among some staff in some schools on other personal matters.

Continuity in the Child's Education

Once the child's illness is diagnosed, like most chronic illnesses there is concern among practitioners working with these children that there is lack of continuity in the child's education. As a result many of these children suffer some isolation from adults and peers and consequent damage to their emotional and psychological development. In looking at models of care used in other countries, we find that efficient short term foster care is well utilized as an appropriate alternative to family care, when this is not available. Once the child has been placed in foster care, he or she should be able to return to the public school system. Given our societal lack of tolerance for differences, however, it would be necessary to put in place public education programmes over a protracted period to ensure that such children would not suffer unduly from further abuse from peers as well as from insensitive members of the community. Such a public education programme must be built into the present training curriculum for teachers, guidance counsellors and allied professionals. The training curriculum should be broadened to include general information on differences among children, which would encompass children with disabilities and children with other chronic illness. Whole modules of this curriculum could be developed using role play, group activities and other media, which could then be used by a variety of practitioners working with children in other situations.

Special Compensation for Foster Parents of Children with AIDS

It is recommended that foster homes and other households providing care for children with special needs be compensated through special grants to enable foster parents to meet their unique demands.

Government Responsibility

Special programmes for children with AIDS could emanate from existing child health welfare programmes within the Children's Services Division and the primary health care system. They must, however, be closely integrated with ongoing public education programmes coming out of those sections of the Ministry of Health dealing with direct health service delivery. This would ensure that through the network of health centres and hospitals, primary health care workers as well as community health aides, there would be national coverage of these children to ensure that assessment, detection and intervention would take place for any child needing such service.

CHILDREN WITH DISABILITIES

Children with disabilities are among the most neglected groups of needy children in Jamaica, in terms of a comprehensive government policy and programme development to ensure that they are able to receive the necessary services to meet their needs. The NGO community has shouldered the responsibility for this sector for some time and consequently there are specific pockets of service delivery which are efficiently run, where mainly international agencies or individuals have stepped in and carved out a niche of services for a particular group. The most widely recognized of these service providers has been The Salvation Army, which has catered to the needs of the blind in Jamaica, and the Sir John Golding Rehabilitation Centre, formerly known as the Mona Rehabilitation Centre, which has catered to the needs of the physically challenged for decades. Apart from these groups there are a number of initiatives, such as the 3-D Projects providing services for children with different kinds of mental deficiencies, and the Jamaica Association for the Deaf, which provides services for the hearing impaired.

Most of these NGO groups perform Herculean tasks with limited resources, and they depend heavily on international donor agencies. Given Jamaica's new-found status in the international donor community as a country which has "passed the worst" in terms of our social development indicators, the reality is that some of these agencies have pulled out or are pulling out of Jamaica, leaving a gaping hole in the NGO community that will have to be filled at least in part by government funds. As we move into the twenty first century these are some of the practical realities that government authorities must address in planning for the social services sector.

Children with Disabilities in Adult Institutions

Another group of children who have traditionally been locked away, neglected and sometimes forgotten are those with disabilities and the mentally ill. Adult institutions like Bellevue Hospital, the major adult mental institution, and some adult infirmaries which house the indigent, have long been dumping grounds for these children. Children with mental and other disabilities are there because of the gaps in the system for detecting and monitoring them at the community and national levels. Children who are mentally ill are in adult institutions because the mental health system has never been designed to create a specific and efficient system for their proper detection and treatment. Autistic children are an example of a group of children in Jamaica who are not catered for in terms of comprehensive government services. There are parents who love their children who are disabled and do not wish them to be institutionalized. These parents need help, but without support they cannot cope with the special needs of these children.

Prevention and Early Detection

If the government of the day is to make a meaningful difference to the situation of children with disabilities, they must operate from a perspective that puts a special emphasis on massive and large scale prevention programmes using systematic and ongoing public education as the vehicle through which essential information on early detection and early intervention is stressed. When one uses a strategy of prevention as the major emphasis of its programme, the advantage is that the scarce human resources that exist in this country in terms of staff for treating children with serious mental and other disabilities can be reserved for children who really need these services. Those children with disabilities who can be managed within their own homes could therefore remain in their families and need not be institutionalized as presently occurs, simply because they are disabled. This would mean that government expenditure could be used in those areas where the resources are most needed, and institutions could move away from being dumping grounds for children with disabilities (see Figure 5.1).

SUMMARY

If one may be guided by history, it may be reasonably assumed that over the next year, some dramatic story about an abused child will be featured in the Jamaican electronic and/or print media more than once. Each time this occurs, there will be a flurry of emotional outcries, some public intellectualizing, then a return to business as usual.

The chapter seeks to analyze the root causes and to offer solutions to manage effectively the problems of child abuse and neglect. It focuses on the problems of children who, for various reasons, are in need of protection. In the first section, some of the basic facts relating to the identification and incidence of child abuse and neglect in Jamaica are presented. This is followed by an analysis of the issues affecting the management of the problem by the social service agencies involved. The problem of children using the transportation system is highlighted and the discussion points to the dangers inherent in a transportation system that has literally become a "killing field" for our children. Suggestions are made as to how the transportation system can be made more "child friendly", and recommendations are made about the use of community based strategies such as the involvement of parents to pressure legislators for changes in policies, which will help to reduce the number of fatalities on our roads generally, and the number of child victims in particular.

The chapter ends with a look at the problem of children who are victims of AIDS and some ethical issues relating to disclosure (in the school setting, for example). It points again to community based intervention to help those children who are victims of the migration process, and it offers possible explanations of the response of children to parental separation.

The policy and programme directions discussed in this chapter are summarized as follows:

- The inclusion of broad based programmes which would include comprehensive public education, parenting education, and prevention. These must be put into place to protect children against domestic violence in particular.
- The need for comprehensive procedural standards of service delivery for all staff working with children and their families, particularly those who

are abused and neglected, via ongoing systematic and cumulative in-house training of all key staff involved. This must be made a priority of government policy and practice. In the case of child abuse and neglect, training materials must be made accessible in the form of a child abuse manual which must be disseminated as an essential working document to all practitioners working in this field, but such a manual must be updated and vetted on a regular basis by all the relevant bodies associated with delivery of services to abused and neglected children.

- Migration counselling for families must be put in place, both for those leaving and those remaining, and should be designed as a part of a national programme to reduce the effects of migration on families. Such a programme could be instituted as part of a cross-cultural exercise and should include orientation programmes in the host country as well as the country of origin.
- There is need for a shift in the orientation of the present child welfare system to include the use of a family preservation model which intervenes in the family before there is family breakdown. There is also need for the system to shift from one of custodial care to one of therapeutic intervention.
- There is need to shift our thinking conceptually and to put our resources into the prevention of the more serious problems of child welfare. That is, focus on children in the community who are at risk (60 percent to 80 percent of our children), thus reducing in the long term, the number of children needing institutionalization and long term care.

NOTES

1. Child Month is set aside in May of each year in Jamaica, as a time when children's service agencies and the society as a whole are asked to focus on children and their needs.
2. Data from the Police Information Centre, Kingston, Jamaica.
3. Data from I. Morrison, *Report of the Task Force on Child Abuse*, Kingston, Jamaica: UNICEF, 1993.

RESOURCE MATERIAL

Books and Documents

Bery, J. 1972. *Social Work with Children.* London: Routledge & Kegan Paul.

Bowlby, J. 1953. *Child Care and the Growth of Love.* London: Pelican Books.

Brodber, E. 1972. *The Abandonment of Children in Jamaica.* Kingston, Jamaica: The Institute of Social and Economic Research, University of the West Indies.

Caribbean Regional Conference Report on Child Abuse and Neglect. 1989. *Child Abuse: Breaking the Cycle.* Port of Spain, Trinidad: UNICEF.

Child Abuse Manual Series: (a) Feller, J., Davidson, H., Harolin, M., Horwits, R. 1992. *Working with the Courts in Child Protection*; (b) Pence, D., Wilson, C. 1992. *Role of Law Enforcement in the Response to Child Abuse and Neglect*; (c) Repanfils, D., Salus, M. 1992. *A Coordinated Response to Child Abuse: A Basic Manual*; (d) Virginia, A., Winn, C. 1992. *Treatment for Abused and Neglected Children: Infancy to Age Eighteen;* Washington, DC: U.S. Department of Health and Human Services.

Cosby, A. 1996. *Stamped Love: The Effects of Parental Migration on Children* (A Study of 15 Adolescent Females). Unpublished study. Kingston, Jamaica: Department of Sociology and Social Work, University of the West Indies, and School of International Training.

Frosh, S., Glaser, D. 1988. *Child Sexual Abuse.* London: MacMillan Education.

Gopaul-McNicol, S. 1992. *Working with West Indian Families.* New York: Guilford Press.

Morrison, I. 1993. *Report of the Task Force on Child Abuse.* Kingston, Jamaica: UNICEF.

Stein, M. 1989. *Adoption and Fostering.* London: MacMillan Education.

Thomas-Hope, E. 1992. *Explanation in Caribbean Migration*, Warwick University Caribbean Studies. London: MacMillan Press.

3-D Projects. 1995. Training Manuals and Video Series. Spanish Town, Jamaica: Pear Tree Press.

Underwood, M., Dunne-Maxim, K. 1993. *Managing Sudden Violent Loss in Schools (A Manual on Adolescent Suicide).* Piscataway, NJ: University of Medicine and Dentistry of New Jersey, Community Mental Health Centre; U.S. Department of Education; U.S. Department of Health and Human Services.

Books for Working with Children

Boulden, J., Boulden, J. 1992. *Secrets that Hurt, Sexual Abuse Activity Book.* New York: Golden Press.

Ernest, K. 1993. *Hope Leaves Jamaica.* London: Methuen Children's Books.

Falcon, D. 1988. *Oscar the Seal: A Story for Children on Sexual Abuse.* New York: Macmillan.

Gray, N. 1978. *Divorce is a Grown-up Problem*. New York: Avon Publishers.

Stetson, J. *Now I Have a Step-parent and it's Kind of Confusing*. New York: Avon Publishers.

AUDIOVISUAL MATERIAL

3-D Projects Video and Manual Series

Parent Training: Training of Parents of Children with Disabilities

Early Detection and Intervention in Childhood Disability: Training the Primary Health Care Workers

The Work Experiences Project: Pre-Vocational Training and Exposure for Young Adults with Disabilities

Income Generating Projects: Self-help for Parents of Children with Disabilities

Assessment of Children with Disabilities: A Guide for the Professional Health Care Worker

Teacher Orientation to Early Childhood Disability: A Practical Guide to Handling the Child with a Disability

REFERRAL SOURCES AND AGENCY CONTACTS

(a) **Child Abuse, Physical, Emotional, Sexual**

The Voluntary Organisation for the Upliftment of Children (VOUCH)
National Heroes Circle
Kingston 4

Child Guidance Clinic
Bustamante Hospital
Arthur Wint Drive
Kingston 5

Child Guidance Clinic
c/o Comprehensive Health Clinic
Slipe Pen Road
Kingston 4

Child Guidance Clinic
c/o Cornwall Regional Hospital
Montego Bay

The Friends Hotline
c/o Jamaica Foundation for Children
119 Old Hope Road
Kingston 6

Mico Youth Counselling
Research and Development Centre
3a Manhattan Road
Kingston 5

(b) **Behavioural Problems, Attention Deficit Disorder, Conduct Disorder, Child Abuse**

Child Health Clinic
c/o Child Health Department
University Hospital of the
West Indies
Kingston 7

(c) **Problems of Migration and Other Interpersonal Difficulties Between Parent and Child, Parenting Training**

Help for Parents
1a Trevennion Park Road
Kingston 5

Parenting Partners
c/o British Save the Children Fund
1 National Heroes Circle
Kingston 4

The Friends Hotline
c/o Jamaica Foundation for Children
119 Old Hope Road
Kingston 6

Coalition for Better Parenting
c/o Ministry of Education,
Youth and Culture
2 National Heroes Circle
Kingston 4

(d) **Group Work with Adolescents, Staff Training for Social Workers and Guidance Counsellors, Parenting Training, Behavioural Problems (in School)**

Mico Youth Counselling Research
and Development Centre
3a Manhattan Road
Kingston 5

(e) **Children with Disabilities and Learning Problems, Parent Education and Training**

3-D Projects Ltd.
42 Trafalgar Road
Kingston 10

Combined Disabilities Association
53 Lyndhurst Road
Kingston 5

Mico Care Centre
3a Manhattan Road
Kingston 5

Salvation Army School for the Blind
57 Mannings Hill Road
Kingston 8

Jamaica Association for the Deaf
9 Marescaux Road
Kingston 5

Jamaica Association for Children
with Learning Disabilities
7 Leinster Road
Kingston 5

Jamaica Association for Mentally
Handicapped Children
c/o School of Hope for
Handicapped Children
7 Golding Avenue
Kingston 7

Centre for HIV, AIDS Research and
Education Services (CHARES)
University Hospital of the West Indies
Mona
Kingston 7

Children
In Trouble

INTRODUCTION

The Children's Defense Fund, one of the strongest child advocacy groups in the United States, describes the historical basis for the special treatment for children in trouble as follows:

> Over 100 years ago, legislation was put in place in the United States of America to ensure that children were treated like children by the legal system. It was assumed at the time that children who break the law, would not be treated as adults. This was partly due to the fact that **children are seen to possess the unique capacity to respond positively to appropriate care and treatment, even moreso than adults.** (Children's Defense Fund 1976)

The fact that this was realized in the United States of America over 120 years ago does not mean that the social planners and policy makers there always deal with children in their country with that maxim in mind, but one gets the impression over the years that some of them do try. Throughout the history of the development of social services for families in Jamaica, very little has been done to improve the quality of service delivery to children in trouble with the law. The result is that they are not treated with the assumption that they can be rehabilitated and returned to their families. Children, despite their fragile nature, are in fact quite resilient and exhibit qualities which suggest that they can become well adjusted, wholesome citizens if they are given the necessary support and encouragement. However, we have a situation where once children get into trouble and they come into contact with the correctional system, they appear to receive a "life sentence" in the form of a Correctional Services order (Cumper 1972) which almost banishes them from their families and communities for most of their childhood years.

INADEQUATE PROGRAMME DEVELOPMENT FOR CHILDREN IN TROUBLE

Many of the children who end up in approved schools (which are really correctional institutions), spend long periods in a facility where there are few programmes designed to cater to their psychological, intellectual, cognitive or physical needs. The lack of these basic services for these children results in a situation where they are put on the road to adult criminal behaviour as a result of being in the institution without adequate programme planning and development. The lack of programme development in this area is due to a number of factors.

Lack of Information Concerning Children and their Welfare

There is a dearth of information in Jamaica (and the rest of the Caribbean) on children and the problems affecting them. When one looks specifically at the factors that cause children to get into trouble, there is little information as to the variables that cause them to end up in a correctional facility. There is also little available information on the geographical regions from which these children come and there is even less information on their family structure and composition. The information that does exist is fragmented; it is not documented in a manner that is easily retrievable and the collection of the information is sporadic and inconsistent. Data collected in this way cannot therefore be used to do systematic planning. We need to have systematic recording of the family profiles on these children by the Department of Correctional Services, so we can better see why they end up in trouble. If a fourteen year old child kills a three year old, or a sixteen year old gunman 'shoots up' a basic school, the society needs to understand why this is happening so that measures can be put into place with our young children who are at risk now, to prevent this from happening with too much frequency in the future.

Predictive Models for Delinquent Behaviour

Predictive models to determine which children are most at risk for the development of delinquent behaviour have already been developed in Jamaica through research coming out of tertiary institutions and these must be used to develop and institute effective policies and programming in this area. One study of Jamaican male adolescents found that some of the factors that were predictive of the development of criminal behaviour included the absence of mother, absence of positive role models, absence of father, number of changes in parental authority figures, and the number of changes in living arrangements (Crawford-Brown 1993). With effective support to families at risk and intensive resocialization programmes for these youngsters, we can make a difference in terms of moving them away from antisocial behaviour. Youngsters in correctional institutions who have committed serious crimes, such as murder, or who have inflicted grievous bodily harm, must be routinely examined and assessed by psychologists to determine their emotional and psychological situation. In addition specially trained clinical social workers could be assigned to work with these youngsters in correctional institutions on an ongoing basis to ensure that they are rehabilitated. It is hoped that the call for a research unit in the Ministry of Security and Justice will materialize and that the mandate of this unit will include the development of a database on children involved in criminal behaviour.

Deficiencies in the Juvenile Justice System

Another factor contributing to the lack of programme development is the fact that the system of juvenile justice has certain loopholes and deficiencies which need to be addressed. For example we need to know why children are put in jails regardless of the laws of the country and we need to know what can be done to prevent this situation from recurring at predictable intervals throughout our nation's history.

Cultural Tolerance

One of the factors that impact on this situation is the apparent cultural tolerance (mentioned earlier in this text) for the abuse of the rights of children. This factor is an important variable within the sociocultural context of child rearing in Jamaica, and is a factor that is further reinforced by specific inefficiencies in the child welfare system which does not have close working relationships with the correctional system for children and youth. Thus the notion that children who get into trouble are "bad" is reflected in the way in which the child welfare and correctional services perceive their roles in terms of helping these children. Historically, children in trouble are given a roof over their heads and other basic necessities until age eighteen and not enough attention is given to rehabilitation, intervention and behaviour modification. Many of these children can be helped through such innovations as *therapeutic foster parenting* or through the use of *teaching parent families*. These programmes focus on helping the children, particularly during the latency stage of development (7-12 years) when they are still able to be resocialized. The use of *behaviour modification* programmes for adolescents through day programmes or within correctional institutions has been found to be effective for working with these children in other countries. Very few attempts have been made to use these alternative programmes of intervention or to adapt them for use in our setting.

The other factor that serves to perpetuate this untenable situation is the fact that Jamaica has had a history of dealing with children in trouble by locking them up, often in adult jails. This reality seems to be tolerated by our society, mainly because this is the way it has been done for years, and because it is felt that there will always be insufficient financial and human resources to improve service delivery in this area. Little attention is paid to the development of alternatives to the incarceration of children, through short term prevention and intervention programmes such as the *Scared Straight Programme*, which attempts to target children who are at risk for criminal behaviour and take them for short visits to prisons, death row, houses of prostitution, abortion clinics, AIDS hospice centres, as a means of scaring them away from antisocial behaviour. Such programmes can be implemented using the existing resources of the correctional services network and the NGO community.

CHILDREN AS PERPETRATORS OF VIOLENCE IN SCHOOLS

It is a widely acknowledged fact that our teachers, particularly those at the secondary level of our education system, have been "given baskets to carry water", and they have often been asked to be all things to all the children that they teach. Apart from being teachers, therefore, they are asked on a daily basis, to be psychiatrists, counsellors, role models, nurses, as well as parents, regardless of their sex. The result of these pressures on our teachers and principals creates social tensions in schools, which have been a major characteristic of our academic communities in the last decade. These tensions no doubt fuel the ongoing untenable state of indiscipline which exists in most of our high and secondary schools. Changes in family structure, resulting in poor parenting, as well as overcrowding, political tribalism, and structural adjustment have been cited by academics as some of the major factors causing this situation. The issue of absent parenting is yet another factor.

Early Detection/Intervention System for Children with Emotional and Behavioural Problems

The need for an early detection system for dealing with emotional and psychological problems within and outside of the school system is a vital part of any effective correctional programme. Such a system must attempt to stop the flow of children coming in from the schools and/or the child welfare system. This can be done through the use of the existing resources within the government and non-government agencies such as the Department of Correctional Services, the Mico Youth Counselling Research and Development Centre and the Child Guidance Clinic network. Behaviour modification and other treatment alternatives are suggested as part of a comprehensive prevention programme which would include an early warning and detection programme within the school system. Such a programme must be designed to identify emotional and behavioural problems before they become intractable during adolescence through the institution of a well trained cadre of guidance counsellors and social workers in the entire school system, including government and private institutions. Such a system would need to have some of the following basic components:

1. A two-tiered level of intervention. This presupposes that the educational system would be provided with technical support at two levels of intervention (see Figure 3.1). At Level I teachers would be supported by guidance counsellors, as is now the case, who would assist with less serious problems relating to adjustment and the normal academic and developmental problems of children and adolescents. At this level additional programmes can be instituted where necessary by the Guidance and Counselling Division of the Ministry, such as mentorship programmes to deal with children at risk for prostitution, or children who are the casualties of serial migration. Socio-educational playgrounds could also be implemented at this level of intervention in select schools to resocialize children and the community using nonacademic instruction through after school and Saturday fun programmes for example, where children can be involved in understanding the teachings of Marcus Garvey, through drama and music, and where elders in the community can pass on the old time values and the oral history which helped to shape our country for centuries. Small community playgrounds are also useful focal points for this kind of activity. At the second level of intervention, Level II, the model suggests that teachers and guidance counsellors may need extra help in assessment and intervention and appropriate referrals and suggests the establishment of a response team, consisting of a clinical psychologist and possibly two graduate level clinical social workers, to go out to the schools on a regular basis to assess and identify children in need of specialized services. The children could then be referred for specialized intervention and treated, if possible within their own homes with parents after school. For uncontrollable behaviour

Fig. 3.1 Model of Early Warning / Detection System
for Children with Emotional / Behavioral Problems

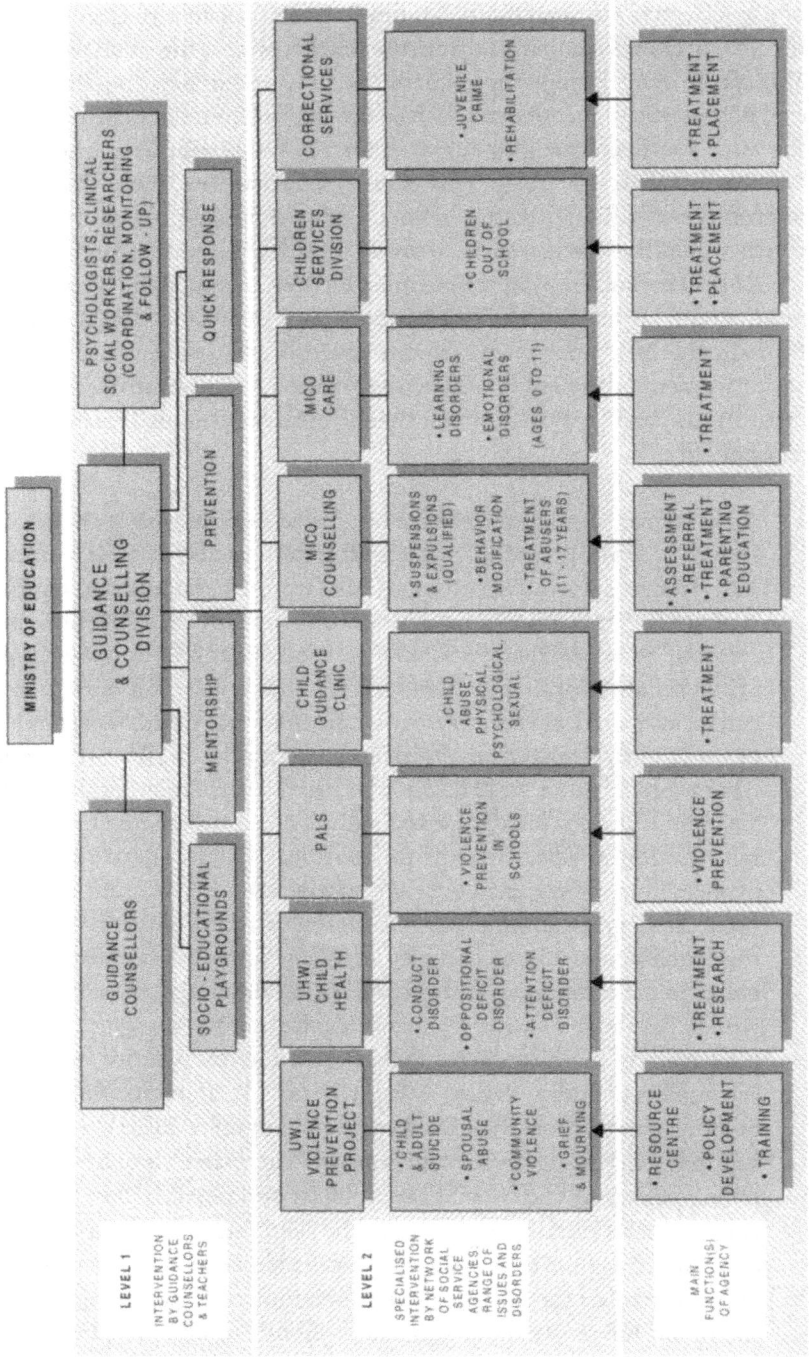

MINISTRY OF EDUCATION

GUIDANCE & COUNSELLING DIVISION

PSYCHOLOGISTS, CLINICAL SOCIAL WORKERS, RESEARCHERS (COORDINATION, MONITORING & FOLLOW - UP)

GUIDANCE COUNSELLORS

SOCIO - EDUCATIONAL PLAYGROUNDS

MENTORSHIP

PREVENTION

QUICK RESPONSE

LEVEL 1

INTERVENTION BY GUIDANCE COUNSELLORS & TEACHERS

CORRECTIONAL SERVICES
• JUVENILE CRIME
• REHABILITATION

CHILDREN SERVICES DIVISION
• CHILDREN OUT OF SCHOOL

MICO CARE
• LEARNING DISORDERS
• EMOTIONAL DISORDERS
(AGES 0 TO 11)

MICO COUNSELLING
• SUSPENSIONS & EXPULSIONS (QUALIFIED)
• BEHAVIOR MODIFICATION
• TREATMENT OF ABUSERS (11 - 17 YEARS)

CHILD GUIDANCE CLINIC
• CHILD ABUSE, PHYSICAL PSYCHOLOGICAL, SEXUAL

PALS
• VIOLENCE PREVENTION IN SCHOOLS

UHWI CHILD HEALTH
• CONDUCT DISORDER
• OPPOSITIONAL DEFICIT DISORDER
• ATTENTION DEFICIT DISORDER

UWI VIOLENCE PREVENTION PROJECT
• CHILD & ADULT SUICIDE
• SPOUSAL ABUSE
• COMMUNITY VIOLENCE
• GRIEF & MOURNING

LEVEL 2

SPECIALISED INTERVENTION BY NETWORK OF SOCIAL SERVICE AGENCIES RANGE OF ISSUES AND DISORDERS

• TREATMENT
• PLACEMENT

• TREATMENT
• PLACEMENT

• TREATMENT

• ASSESSMENT
• REFERRAL
• TREATMENT
• PARENTING EDUCATION

• TREATMENT

• VIOLENCE PREVENTION

• TREATMENT
• RESEARCH

• RESOURCE CENTRE
• POLICY DEVELOPMENT
• TRAINING

MAIN FUNCTION(S) OF AGENCY

and violent and aggressive behaviour children who are suspended from school could be referred to a day treatment facility like the Mico Counselling Centre as part of their "suspension activity package". If the child does not attend for treatment he or she would not be allowed to return to school. In this way teachers could be given a chance to teach and children and parents could be helped before it is too late. Children who need other kinds of treatment such as medical intervention could be quickly diagnosed and referred with minimum disruption to the child's education.

2. A mobile response unit. Level II intervention can be done through the establishment of a small mobile response unit made up of well trained clinical social workers and a clinical psychologist who would be able to go out regularly to the schools at the regional level to do assessments and make recommendations for intervention. When adolescents are identified as presenting with behavioural problems which affect their functioning at school they must be assisted with their families to receive intervention through day treatment programmes from their homes. NGOs and private organizations already provide some of these services. Within such a system they would be expected to work as a team to support the teachers and guidance counsellors rather than see themselves as individual agencies within their prescribed territorial boundaries. Given our historical tendencies to keep our services and programmes in well defined "packages", and our overwhelming need for human and material resources in this area, one would have to develop well defined and well established systems of referral.

3. A method of referral. Parents and children could call treatment centres directly, or be referred by their school principal, guidance counsellor, or a social worker from a social service agency. Unfortunately, many parents do not use these services as there is a reluctance to accept counselling services as part of the support system that they need to cope with the task of parenting. Despite this, many agencies are overburdened due to a lack of funding. Given the pull out of some international donor agencies and given our new status as a country that has good scores in terms of our infant mortality rates and infant immunization coverage, the government of the day must make provision to pick up the slack in terms of funding these vital NGO agencies now providing these all important services. It is also important in attempting to set up such a system, or alternative systems, to be aware that adolescents do not always present with behavioural problems by acting violently and aggressively. Some children become depressed, and some children present with suicidal ideation. All of these behaviours must

be managed and treated within a comprehensive system which does not allow any child to fall through the cracks.

Depression as Acting-Out Behaviour in Children

Guidance counsellors and principals know that many of our children are acting out because they are depressed. Some of them are depressed because they are victims of migration. Some of them are acting aggressively because they have been physically and sexually abused. There are a variety of factors. The problem is, however, that no matter how caring and hardworking, the normal teacher does not have the time to be a therapist to these children and our present cadre of guidance counsellors do not possess the necessary skills to implement the long term behaviour modification that is needed in many of the cases.

The question is, therefore, what does a society do with children who are too violent and aggressive and antisocial to fit into the school system? What do we do with youth who are too disruptive, smart or cocky, or too withdrawn and depressed to work along with others in the classroom? The answer is to identify the problems early and intervene with the child and the family through the existing network of social service agencies, but rather than leave it up to the ingenuity of one particular parent or another, there needs to be a system in place (which is known and used by the educational community as a resource), which would allow them to teach in an atmosphere that is more conducive to learning than is presently the case.

CHILDREN IN ADULT JAILS

The problem of children in adult jails is another problem that remains in place because we accept that as a society this is the best that we have to offer our children. The following discussion explores these issues.

One of the most glaring weaknesses of Jamaican society is the seeming inability to take care of and protect children according to the most basic international, regional or national standards. In the case of our so called "normal" child population, we are adept at abusing them (physically, sexually and institutionally), and then we provide few workable systems for either healing or redress.

One of the manifestations of institutional abuse is the fact that several of our children each year are interned in jails because of a shortage of child care facilities. In mid-1994 one popular radio talk show host interviewed a representative of the New York-based Human Rights Watch group regarding a report done by that individual on children in jails in Jamaica. Comments on the major issues that came out of that discussion reflected some of our societal attitudes to children and were very revealing.

Do Foreigners Care More About our Children?

The overall tone of the interview suggested that in Jamaica we feel that it is satisfactory for children to be in jail and the impression was that Jamaicans felt that too much was being made of the children's situation by the international children's rights group. "After all", said one commentator, "standards in the developed world are higher than those in the developing world"! The US children's rights activist responded rather indelicately by stating that standards anywhere in the world would dictate that children should not be placed in any location where human faeces were running through their place of abode.

One experienced a feeling of shame and mortification on hearing this interview, not because of the content of the disclosures, but because we came across as a people who do not care about our children, and that is untrue. The developed world (correctly or incorrectly) already considers us to be incompetent in almost every aspect of managing our society. We would look much better as a people if we at least acknowledged to ourselves and to the international community that the way we treat our children leaves much to be desired. Children should not be in jail. This is a matter that should be addressed at the highest levels of our society and is an important part of the self-awareness that we need to establish as we move along the road to maturity as a society.

Local Advocacy

The second aspect of this discussion of concern was that the local commentators did not include in their discussion a voice from the local child advocacy community, which has been calling for years, like the proverbial "pelicans in the wilderness", for attention to be paid to the way our children are treated. In fact, the problem of children in jail was a major child advocacy issue in the 1970s, when *The Jamaica Daily News* in the column "Our Children Now", written by Peter Maxwell in the 1970s, led a campaign with the assistance of VOUCH to get children out of jail in Jamaica. Twenty years later local advocates are still fighting the same issue. It seems that the powers that be only listen if the voices that speak out for our children are foreign ones. It also seems that the society continues to undervalue the technical expertise available in Jamaica, particularly in the area of research on child welfare as well as programme and policy development. It is only when the lights of the international community shine into the darkest corners of our society that we temporarily pay attention. The only glimmer of hope that seems to have come from this situation is the temporary embarrassment that such a situation created - the hope is that this embarrassment will one day materialize into action.

How Do we Keep Children Out of Adult Jails?

There is a suggestion that the problem of children in jail in Jamaica is due to overcrowding in places of safety. The government's knee-jerk response to this is typically to express the need to build more and more places of safety to house these children. However this is just one response to the problem and it is not the most cost effective. The problem is a complex one and must be addressed in relation to the specific problems bringing these children into the country's child welfare and correctional system. The solutions require strong support at the policy making and highest administrative levels of the Children's Services Division, the Child Support Unit, and the Department of Correctional Services.

Structural Problems in Child Welfare and Correctional Systems

The central question that emerges in a discussion of the issue of children in lock-ups in Jamaica is this: even if international standards did not exist, and even if there were no International Charter on the Rights of the Child, don't we know that it is wrong to lock up our children in prisons with adults? Don't we know that it is wrong to put our children in prisons that we all know are almost medieval in terms of their conditions and standards? Of course we all know this, but year after year, scores of our children end up in police lock-ups. Why do we allow this and other atrocities to exist year after year?

The reasons are based on structural problems in an inefficient and poorly managed child welfare system, as well as societal and cultural complacency. The result is the absence of a working policy that can be operationalized at all levels of the child welfare system. A policy must focus on children and families in an integrated manner which builds bridges across the different social agencies involved with children. This is a basic prerequisite in any society that hopes to progress in terms of providing a social safety net to deal with the economic realities of structural adjustment.

Children in Jail: Push Factors

The main cause of children being placed in police lock-ups is the fact that places of safety, which were set up as temporary shelters in the child welfare system, are overcrowded. This problem was highlighted in 1994 when an adolescent girl, aged 11, was raped in a police station while awaiting a transfer to a place of safety. The government's usual response to this problem is to assume that we need more institutions, particularly remand centres and children's homes. The argument which follows from this is that there is no more money, hence nothing more can be done.

However, more buildings will not necessarily solve the problem. As discussed in chapter 1, overcrowding in places of safety occurs because there are serious deficiencies in the channels through which children ought to be exiting from these temporary institutions. One place of safety built to house a maximum of ninety children is made to house up to twice that number on occasion. On the other hand, some institutions, particularly children's homes, do not have their full capacity.

As shown in Figure 1.3, overcrowding can occur when there is a blockage in the channels of exit from places of safety. There is no policy that even attempts to take children out of places of safety and children's homes and put them back into their own homes. There is no policy that aggressively attempts to get them adopted or fostered. Thus, once a child is placed in a children's home, that child often remains there until age eighteen, regardless of the ability of his or her family to take the child back.

Solutions can therefore be found for the problem of overcrowding in places of safety and other institutions if we use a family reunification model[1] or adaptations of it, rather than a family *dissolution* model, on which our present system seems to be based. We could actually strengthen families in the process of taking care of our children's needs. This would mean that the needs of the two main groups of children under government care (children in trouble with the law and children in need of care and protection) would be dealt with at their source, which is in the family, rather than depend solely on the expensive method of institutionalization, which often leaves children experiencing emotional and psychological problems rooted in bitterness and resentment toward their families. The result is that these children often become dysfunctional in terms of their own roles as parents.

What Needs to be Done

- Each child who enters the correctional system or the child welfare system must be evaluated in three ways, namely psychologically, socially and academically, to determine individual and family strengths and weaknesses. Once this is done, a short term treatment plan should determine the best placement options, which may include short term institutionalization, skills training, group/individual therapy or family therapy. Such a treatment plan must be developed to include the involvement of parents and/or other key family members. This type of programme would effectively screen and deal quickly with cases where there are minor infractions of the law and emphasize training in the home environment.

- Serious attention must be given to upgrading the approved schools and children's homes, and operating them as specialized treatment facilities for the cases of hard core juvenile delinquents or cases where family treatment is not possible. Treatment could include skills training at the crux of a behaviour modification programme for children with behavioural problems. Group and individual therapy would also be emphasized. Trained psychologists, social workers and other staff would be required to make this programme effective and, given the shortage of these human resources, the services could be structured on a regional basis initially, with trained personnel being made available to visit these institutions at predictable intervals for assessment and follow up treatment.

- All children in institutions, therefore, whether places of safety, children's homes or correctional institutions for children and adolescents, must have assessment and treatment programmes designed to work with children according to their needs. Children in the correctional system and child welfare system must have the option of returning to a home environment where they can receive family therapy or other material support, if necessary. With welfare reform now being discussed as a new aspect of government policy, it is time that welfare programmes be designed to provide some support for families of children in government care to make it possible for these children to be returned to a home environment under the supervision of trained welfare officers, rather than being placed in a badly run institution. It is important to note that well run institutions should be strengthened and developed as treatment centres for children with specialized needs, such as uncontrollable children or children with conduct disorders.

- Government agencies must reexamine and reorganize the channels of communication between the police, the Department of Correctional Services, and the Children's Services Division of the Ministry of Health, to ensure that extensive collaboration exists at all levels of the service.

- Clear and concise manuals on codes of conduct and administrative procedures relating to the management of children in correctional institutions must be written and made available to all correctional institutions and agencies working with children.

- Appropriate training must be put in place to ensure that these administrative procedures are compatible with the new children's policies that are presently being drafted. There should be clear operational procedures regarding the interface between the child welfare system and the correctional system. These two agencies must work closely to avoid the almost predictable trek in some instances of children from foster care to child care institution to correctional institution to adult jails. Morrison (1995) documents this process graphically in his anecdotal monograph "Teach Me a Better Way to Live".

Managing Violent and Aggressive Youths in the Correctional Services System

Manuals coming out of the section of the correctional services that caters to youth should include specific information on how to manage and treat behavioural problems, particularly uncontrollable behaviour requiring the use of restraints within the correctional facility. Children and youth who exhibit boisterous behaviour should not be dealt with by physical punishment as is now the case, as was reported recently in the press by the adolescents themselves. Many staffers resort to physical punishment because they know of few alternatives. We have to retool and retrain staffers as to the relevant practices that are useful and appropriate for working with difficult teenagers. We cannot continue to beat them into submission, as it only introduces hostility and resentment which exacerbates the tremendous levels of violence that already exist in the society. Other policies should dictate how to deal with violent and aggressive children inside and outside of the institution, by using the simple tried and true method of reward and punishment. These models of intervention are well documented and used throughout the world, and there is no reason for us to continue the use of antiquated child management practices which have failed to produce the model children we think we would like to see coming out of our correctional facilities. The lack of these vital inputs has created a sense of stagnation within the youth correctional services which has gone on for years and has engendered frustration at all levels, and there is a feeling across the system that there is a lack of political will on the part of succeeding governments to deal with this issue in a rational and professional manner. There is also a seeming lack of an understanding of the relationship between untreated aggressive adolescents and violent adult criminals.

We cannot continue to pour millions of dollars into youth correctional facilities in the current fashion. These institutions simply absorb financial input like sponges while the children leave just as damaged as they entered, without any real prospects for their future.

Above are some of the policy issues that must be dealt with if the problem of children in lock-ups is to be tackled in some systematic way. Until these matters are addressed with the financial support that they deserve, we will be continually fending off the glare of national and international publicity, trying to rescue our economy and our tourism industry as the scourge of violence wreaks havoc on our agencies of socialization.

STREET AND WORKING CHILDREN IN JAMAICA

Regardless of the dismal economic climate existing in Jamaica throughout the year, the sights and sounds of Christmas are alive and well year after year. As the hustle and bustle of the season sets in, some of the most enduring impressions of Christmas time in urban Jamaica are those of our children who work. Working children are everywhere. At that time, children can be seen "hustling" on almost every street corner, peddling pillows, artificial flowers, starlights, balloons and other paraphernalia which are part of the excitement and noise of our Jamaican Yuletide season. Other children as young as six and seven years old, many of them girls, sell fruits, toys, clothing, everything but the kitchen sink. Given the latest UNICEF figures on working children in Jamaica, which puts the total number of working children at 23,000, children represent a significant part of the Jamaican labour force, particularly in the urban area. As the malls open later during holidays and on weekends, a common sight at nights is the picture of dozens of desperate-looking children selling and begging for their supper, often barefooted and hungry, many times unaccompanied by an adult.

Characteristics of Street and Working Children in Jamaica: Push Factors

Recently, there was an incident in St Thomas when a baby, no more than two years old, was seen in dirty diapers at the side of a dangerous highway begging for money with his mother urging him on from a hidden enclosure a few feet away. The reality is that as times get harder, children are increasingly brought into the labour force and are required to work for longer hours to support themselves and others in their household. The worrying factor is that our social scientists tell us that street children who work in this manner are not without parents as occurs for example in the bustling cities of South America, but are sent out by their parents to fend for themselves (Ennew 1986; Crawford-Brown 1994). There are, however, specific factors that are pushing our children into the streets. These are shown in Figure 3.2.

Working Children: Vital to Economic Survival of Inner City Households

One mother interviewed remarked that her sales increased by as much as 20 percent per week when her eleven year old son does the "hustling." This was

Fig.3.2 Model Showing Factors that Cause Children to Work in Jamaica

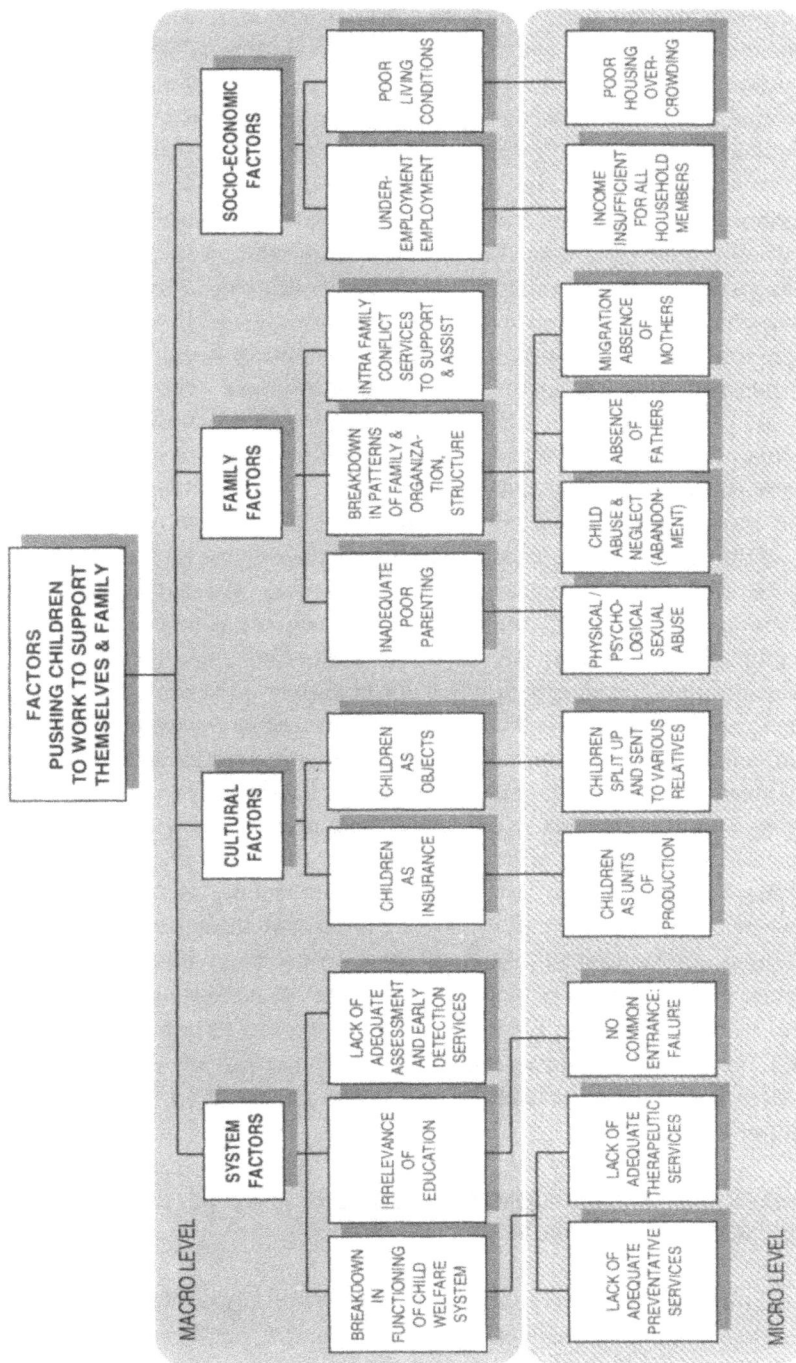

FACTORS PUSHING CHILDREN TO WORK TO SUPPORT THEMSELVES & FAMILY

MACRO LEVEL

SYSTEM FACTORS
- BREAKDOWN IN FUNCTIONING OF CHILD WELFARE SYSTEM
- IRRELEVANCE OF EDUCATION
- LACK OF ADEQUATE ASSESSMENT AND EARLY DETECTION SERVICES

CULTURAL FACTORS
- CHILDREN AS INSURANCE
- CHILDREN AS OBJECTS

FAMILY FACTORS
- INADEQUATE POOR PARENTING
- BREAKDOWN IN PATTERNS OF FAMILY & ORGANIZATION, STRUCTURE
- INTRA FAMILY CONFLICT SERVICES TO SUPPORT & ASSIST

SOCIO-ECONOMIC FACTORS
- UNDER-EMPLOYMENT EMPLOYMENT
- POOR LIVING CONDITIONS

MICRO LEVEL

- LACK OF ADEQUATE PREVENTATIVE SERVICES
- LACK OF ADEQUATE THERAPEUTIC SERVICES
- NO COMMON ENTRANCE: FAILURE
- CHILDREN AS UNITS OF PRODUCTION
- CHILDREN SPLIT UP AND SENT TO VARIOUS RELATIVES
- PHYSICAL / PSYCHO-LOGICAL SEXUAL ABUSE
- CHILD ABUSE & NEGLECT (ABANDON-MENT)
- ABSENCE OF FATHERS
- MIGRATION ABSENCE OF MOTHERS
- INCOME INSUFFICIENT FOR ALL HOUSEHOLD MEMBERS
- POOR HOUSING OVER-CROWDING

her justification for withdrawing him from school, and she could not be described by any means as a wicked, cruel or neglectful mother. The harsh reality of her situation is that as a domestic helper who earned a minimum wage, she had to include her eleven year old son's income in her weekly budget, otherwise she could not afford to pay her rent, and to meet her grocery bill for herself and five children. Putting up centres for street children and setting up high-level committees for addressing the problems of working children are useful strategies in the short term, but unless we put in place preventive programmes that tackle the root causes, and the underlying factors pushing the children onto the streets, these eleven year old hustlers, some of whom have sales techniques that could rival that of any million-dollar insurance salesperson, will be joining the ranks of the criminal gangs by the time another Christmas comes around.

The point is that we will never be able to build enough drop-in centres to hold and house all our street children. The idea therefore is not to keep building more and more institutions to house our children but to help their families, and enable and empower them to take care of their own.

Within one year the eleven year old mentioned above had changed from a polite, disciplined youngster to a young member of a budding criminal gang. The mother fought tooth and nail with the help of the Family Court to keep her family together, without success. If the Family Court had the support of a good prevention programme for adolescents on the verge of criminal activity, through the Correctional Services Division, or if the practitioner working with this family had access to information on how to help young adolescents at risk for gang involvement, that child might have been saved. If that mother could have received a little help just to keep her afloat, a little help with a bed so he could be close to her, a little help with some seed money to relaunch her higglering business so he could go to school, instead of selling on the street, she might have been able to save him. Where is our sense of direction? Are we going to go the route of the Central American cities where street children are killed as a means of ridding the city of the inconvenience? Our street children have families. Our street children are there because their families cannot cope. Why can't we help families who will then help their own children? Where are our priorities? Will it be punishment and incarceration or can it be support and family empowerment?

CHILDREN WHO ARE CRIMINALS/CHILDREN WHO EXHIBIT ANTISOCIAL BEHAVIOUR

It is often said that the Jamaican society is full of people who talk too much and do too little. We have conferences, seminars, and workshops *ad infinitum*, about everything under the sun. We discuss and we analyse social issues *ad nauseam* and yet we still do not seem to be able to come to grips with some of the fundamental problems affecting our society. The social situation of our children, particularly those who commit serious crimes, is one such problem. Since the beginning of the 1990s, children have been killed in increasing numbers. They have been killed by policemen, gunmen, minibus drivers, parents, guardians and even by their peers. The solutions to these problems continue to be addressed in a piecemeal fashion as overworked social agencies fight to continue their funding from year to year. In addition, adequate data collection systems still do not exist in the child welfare and juvenile correctional agencies and so when the spectre of juvenile crime rears its ugly head, we are all alarmed and seemingly unprepared. Existing and available data are not used to create the necessary link between policy and programme development. In the area of juvenile delinquency for example, one finds that the social research produced by our universities and other institutions is not used and integrated with appropriate programmes and policies. The abandonment of·children, for example, is a social issue that has been researched and analysed since the 1970s in work by Erna Brodber. Prescriptions for programmes and policies have been documented and published through the Institute of Social and Economic Research at the University of the West Indies, but there is no single unit of the Children's Services Division (the main child welfare agency) which seeks to analyse social data relating to children, and put these findings into policy and programme planning.

The Community " Don": One of the New Agents of Socialization

The Recruitment Drive for Young Boys for the Criminal Gang

A fourteen year old from the inner-city reported to the Children's Lobby recently that he was forced to watch the gang rape of a young teenaged girl by community dons because he was seen as "soft" by the dons and needed to be "hardened". He was forced to watch this horrible activity in his own community. He told us of the process by which numerous seven or eight year old boys were socialized by the dons. When one mother attempted to discipline her child, for doing something wrong, she was admonished by the don who said, "No mada, we have 'im in training, you no deal with 'im, leave that to we". If we leave socialization of our children to the dons, we will have no country left in a very short time.

Young Girls for the Don's Pleasure

Clients attending the University of the West Indies Violence Prevention Family Clinic in the Department of Sociology and Social Work suggest that mothers in the inner city are asked regularly to send their girls as young as 12 -16 years old to sleep with the community don for his pleasure. If they refuse the family can be burnt out, or somehow chased from the community. Girls socialized in this way are affected for years, as many young girls act out in violent and aggressive ways by running away, or by exhibiting sexual behaviour which seems to exhibit a lack of judgement. These problems are often difficult to manage and treat and require careful and skilled intervention.

Mothers and children mentioned the fact that the dons and other criminals had a special liking for girls who had passed their Common Entrance examinations and were attending high schools. The implications of these actions have serious consequences for the life of many communities and the life of the nation. We have to spend our resources on these families to help them, support them and to help them to cope. Instead, we prefer to spend the little money we have on putting the casualties of these situations in children's homes or approved schools from which they may run away to return to the streets, or to spend money to keep them in prisons or mental institutions when they become adults.

Adolescent Males and Crime: Juvenile Correctional Service Reform

The latest realization from police records is that adolescent males are involved in some of the most brutal crimes in our country. What does the research suggest about the social factors associated with this problem? In a comparative study of 140 conduct-disordered and non-conduct-disordered adolescents (Crawford-Brown 1993), one of the most significant factors associated with what one could term serious delinquency was the absence of mothers from the homes. Factors associated with the absence of mothers were primarily death or migration.

One important conclusion of this research was that there was a dire need for family service agencies to be made available to rural and urban families. As many as 30 percent of the sample of the boys in one major correctional facility were from the rural areas. The social agencies working with these children need to provide strong material as well as psychological support in the form of ongoing counselling which must be accessible and available in rural and urban parishes as well as welfare grants to ensure that alternate family support systems are strengthened before there is total family breakdown. This kind of comprehensive "programmatic coverage" involving existing resources within the correctional services pool of probation officers would require a rethinking of the role and function of the present children and youth correctional facilities, and its supporting agencies, so that they offer a comprehensive preventive focus rather than the present focus on mainly custodial care, after there is family breakdown and the child becomes delinquent, or exhibits some other form of antisocial behaviour.

Need for Further Research

Further research that can credibly inform the development of appropriate social policy in this area is to be encouraged in order to develop our pool of information regarding the problem. This is the direction in which we should be going. Sensational journalism or wringing of hands in despair and consternation will not make this problem go away. We must look at the underlying social issues through systematic social research and deal with them in a comprehensive and aggressive manner using innovative approaches. Failure to do this now may result in an unmanageable whirlwind of delinquency and its companion symptom, adult crime.

SUMMARY

This chapter looks at the difficult situation of children in Jamaica who have been in trouble with the law. In a recently published book, written by a "survivor" of the Jamaican child welfare system, entitled "Teach Me a Better Way to Live", the author recounts the traumatic experience of a child who, through parenting deficiencies, was thrown into the correctional system in Jamaica (Morrison 1995). This account also illustrates the fact that there are many difficult situations that children can get into in the child welfare system. The consequences of these can haunt them for the rest of their lives.

This chapter also looks at factors pushing children into the streets and highlights the consequent potential for criminal activity. It makes the point that agencies working with children on the streets need not seek to create new organizational structures to deal with these children. That approach would not address the root causes of this phenomenon. The agencies must work with the home while intervening on the streets.

The chapter also points to a range of factors affecting the delivery of services to children in trouble with the law. The section on children in jail focuses on the recurrent problem of children being held behind bars in Jamaica, and it points to the problem of overcrowding in places of safety and children's homes as the major reason that authorities give for this chronic problem. This chapter suggests that those in authority have become callous about the issue, and need to operate from the assumption that each child is a special individual, coming out of a unique family situation, and he or she must be treated accordingly.

The following recommendations are therefore put forward:

* The present system must expand its role and function to include assessment and the early detection of children with emotional and behavioural problems both inside and outside of the educational system.

- There is need to restructure the child welfare system to include a preventive component which would deal with the problems of the family before there is a breakdown.
- There also needs to be specialized units within the Children Services Division which would focus on prevention, protection, and alternative care, as well as research and evaluation (see Figure 1.4). Within such a structure, the Alternative Care Division could have direct links to the Department of Correctional Services, and all institutions would be required to be certified based on international standards proposed for all children institutions. Training for these institutions could then be standardized by one agency using the "old" National Children's Home training model, where one or two good institutions could be used as models to train the others. This kind of approach can work if we try working together, pooling our scarce resources, as a team of agencies rather than as separate entities.

Community Violence and Children

For some time the Jamaican urban environment has been plagued by violent crimes. Presently, the nation is embroiled in a verbal conflagration over what is to be done to address the problems of crime and violence. In these discussions, very often little is said about the children who are battle-scarred and battle-weary as a result of the trauma of gun violence. Many years after the event, these children are still traumatized, to the point where their academic progress is affected and their ability to relate interpersonally with others is irreparably damaged. Apart from this fact, children who grow up with ongoing violence come to see violence as a way of life and produce dysfunctional families of their own, thus perpetuating the violence.

Help the Schools: Regional Response Teams

Violence in the schools feeds on violence in the community. Let us have preventive and therapeutic programmes in the schools supported by teams of trained psychologists and clinical social workers, operating on a regional basis to help the children and teachers cope with this scourge of violence (see Figure 3.1). Let us not wait until these children become adults. By then it will be too late. By detecting violence in the school system, we can pick up problems related to children and violence in the community.

What Needs to Be Done

We need to use up our existing system of community based facilities which must work in conjunction with the education authorities. These facilities must offer intensive counselling in a residential programme for more seriously disturbed children, and nonresidential, day programmes for those who have emotional or conduct behaviour problems.

In September 1994, the Mico Youth Counselling Centre started offering a range of day and evening programmes for parents, children, and adolescents (within or outside of the educational system) who have emotional and/or behavioural problems. Other agencies, such as the Child Health Department of the University of the West Indies and The Child Guidance Clinic network, offer ongoing assessment, as well as some individual intervention for children. Other NGOs, such as the British Save the Children Fund (Jamaica), Canadian Save the Children Fund (CANSAVE) and VOUCH also offer ongoing programmes to assess and treat children experiencing a variety of emotional and behavioural problems. These agencies should be accessed as soon as children present a problem, not years afterwards when little can be done. The different agencies must be made to see themselves as part of a comprehensive system working toward a common goal, not as individual agencies doing their work in an isolated and piecemeal fashion, but as viable organizations working to provide comprehensive services delivery to the child and family. Such a system is presented graphically in this chapter, and is included to encourage discussion among practitioners and policy makers, and to provide a possible research agenda for those seeking solutions to this seemingly intractable problem.

NOTE

1. Family reunification is a policy which presupposes that with support deficient families can be empowered to take care of their children. It assumes that it is more cost effective to bring up children in their own homes than in other forms of alternate care. Thus, resources are put into reuniting families and giving them the resources to help them manage without prolonged institutionalization.

RESOURCE MATERIAL

Books and Documents

Dumont, B.E., Altesman, R.I. 1986. *A Parent's Guide to Teens andCults*. New Jersey: PIA Press.

Ennew, J. 1986. *Street and Working Children, A Guide to Planning*. Development Manual 4. London: Save the Children U.K.

Kadushin, A. 1969. *Adopting Older Children*. New York: Columbia University Press.

Morrison, L.J. 1995. *Teach me a Better Way to Live*. Kingston, Jamaica: G & M Associates.

Underwood, M.M., Dunne-Maxim, K. 1993. *Managing Sudden Violent Loss in the Schools (Suicide in Schools)*. New Jersey: University of Medicine and Dentistry.

Walker, A. 1967. *Case-work in Residential Schools for Disturbed Children*. Case Conferences, Vol. 13.

Walker, A. 1968. *Social Influences on Disturbed Immigrant Children*. Case Conferences, Vol. 13, No. 6.

Wolff, S. 1969. *Children Under Stress*. London: Penguin Books.

Wycoff, P. 1988. *Children in Violent Families*. New York: Macmillan.

Audiovisual Material

Caribbean Media Services. 1987. *Children at Risk in Jamaica*. Kingston, Jamaica: The Children's Lobby.

Caribbean Media Services. 1997. *Talk it Out, Don't Fight it Out*. Kingston, Jamaica: Child Month Committee.

Audiovisual Production. 1995. *Sexual Abuse in Jamaica*. Kingston, Jamaica: Caribbean Child Development Centre.

Referral Sources and Agency Contacts

(a) Children in Trouble

Department of Correctional Services
Head Office
5 King Street
Kingston

Department of Correctional Services, Probation Office
12 Ocean Boulevard
Kingston

Department of Correctional Services, Regional Offices (Area Offices)
Highgate Probation Office
Highgate PO
St Mary

Mandeville Probation Office
1B Wesley Road
Mandeville PO

May Pen Probation Office
10 March Road

May Pen PO
Clarendon

(b) **Street and Working Children**

LEAP (Learning for Earning Activity
Programme)
2 National Heroes Circle,
and 115 Duke Street
Kingston 4

British Save the Children Fund
1 National Heroes Circle
Kingston 4

YMCA (Young Men's
Christian Association)
Hope Road
Kingston 10

(c) **Domestic Violence - Children and
Families; Effects of Violence
on Children**

Women's Crisis Centre
18 Ripon Road
Kingston 5

Child and Family Clinic
c/o Violence Prevention Programme
Department of Sociology
and Social Work
Social Science Faculty
University of the West Indies
Kingston 7

Family Life Ministries
14 West Avenue
Kingston 8

Bethel Counselling Centre
c/o Bethel Baptist Church
Hope Road
Kingston 10

Webster Counselling Centre
c/o Webster United Church
Half Way Tree Road
Kingston 10

Fathers Incorporated
56 Old Hope Road
Kingston 5

(d) **Children in Jail**

Police Community
Relations Division
Ruthven Road
Kingston 10

Voluntary Organization for
the Upliftment of Children
(VOUCH)
1 National Heroes Circle
Kingston 4

(e) **Violence in Schools**

Guidance and Counselling Division
Ministry of Education,
Youth and Culture
Canewood Centre
37 Arnold Road
Kingston 4

PALS (Peace and Love in
Schools [Elementary
School Age])
c/o Ministry of Education,
Youth and Culture
2 National Heroes Circle
Kingston 4

Dispute Resolution
Foundation Ltd. (Adolescents
and Adults)
32½ Duke Street, 7th Floor
Kingston

Mico Youth Counselling
Research and Development
Centre
3a Manhattan Road
Kingston 5

Major Craig's Drug
Centre (Drop-in Facility)
57 Peter's Lane
Kingston

(f) **Grief, Mourning and
Loss, Chronic Illness, the Dying
Child, Helping Families
Cope With Sudden Loss**

The Family Centre
Social Work Unit
University Hospital of the
West Indies
Kingston 7

Medical Social Work Department
University Hospital of the
West Indies
Golding Avenue
Kingston 7

Psychiatric Department
Cornwall Regional Hospital
Montego Bay

(g) **Counselling and
Rehabilitation Services for
Drug Abuse and Addiction**

National Council on Drug Abuse
2 Melmac Avenue
Kingston 5

Treatment Centres:

Patricia House
6 Upper Musgrave Avenue
Kingston 10

Addiction Alert Drug
Counselling Service
57 East Street
Kingston

4

Parenting
in the
Jamaican
Society

INTRODUCTION

Over the past decade an international focus on children's rights by the United Nations has turned public attention to child rearing styles and practices all over the world. In looking at child rearing styles and practices in the Caribbean over the years we know that there is a tendency for Caribbean parents to use physical punishment as the main method of disciplining children and it is widely accepted in the region as an integral aspect of child rearing. In Jamaica one of the interesting findings relating to the abuse of children is that the largest group of children who are the victims of sexual abuse is between the ages of six and eight years (Survey of Services for Children 1986; Child Guidance Clinic 1994).

Another finding (Milbourne 1989) suggests that boys are physically abused more than girls, and girls are sexually abused much more than boys are (see Figures 2.1 and 2.2). This has serious implications for parenting, and is a reflection of the societal values around child rearing.

Another parenting problem affecting the children of Jamaica is the issue of the effect of violence and the increasing levels of sexualization of children and young people in the media. The matter of parenting after divorce, the issue of discipline and punishment, as well as the challenge of how to deal practically with domestic violence, are all matters of concern to many Jamaican parents. This chapter looks at some of the most worrying of these parenting issues, and offers simple and effective options for dealing with them.

DOMESTIC VIOLENCE AND CHILDREN

The controversy that accompanied the passage of the Domestic Violence Act in Jamaica focused on the need to address deficiencies suggested by various women's organizations, opinion leaders and concerned citizens. Discussions, by and large, dealt with the shortcomings of the Act as they related to women. However, the voices that speak on behalf of the Jamaican child were not as prominent as one would have expected, given the level of domestic violence perpetrated against this very vulnerable section of our population. There is more than ample grounds for concern here. Some of this concern is reflected in discussions that one finds in the literature on child welfare that speak specifically to the question of children caught in the web of domestic violence, especially in situations where both mother and children have to be removed from the home.

Contemporary child care practice increasingly tends to adopt the strategy of keeping mother and children together in specially designed shelters when there is violence in the home. At present, there is only one shelter in Jamaica (located in Kingston) that is set up to accommodate a mother and her children who have to flee their home on account of domestic violence. What kind of counselling and assessment facilities are provided for these children in terms of their emotional and psychological status? What does the new law say about this very important feature of our domestic violence programme? What is the policy framework behind this legislation, in terms of the provision of shelters on a nationwide basis?

A second issue concerns the relationship between the Domestic Violence Act and existing legislation. Removal of children from their homes for their own protection is currently guided by the Child Care and Protection Act. There are implications for this Act *vis-à-vis* the Domestic Violence Act, when cases involving the removal of parent and child are to be adjudicated. The new Act must address the plight of both mother and children who are forced to leave their family home and remain in shelter for a prolonged period. There is a distinct need for legislators to collaborate with child welfare practitioners and planners so that these two pieces of legislation are coherent, and the programmes to back up the legislation are well planned and integrated, within the limits of our resources and capabilities. Another important aspect of the law concerns treatment of the abuser, an issue which has been consistently ignored by programme and policy makers over the years.

Treating the Abuser - Mandatory Counselling or Jail Sentences

One model for treating the abuser that is widely used quite successfully in the developed world, particularly in North America, links mandatory counselling to jail sentences, using the administrative infrastructure of agencies similar to the Correctional Services Division, as well as NGOs. This system works very effectively to force abusers to become involved in individual and group counselling for a sustained period, and it has proven to be a useful sentencing option. It would seem that this is a pragmatic alternative that would need to be addressed in the legislation if we plan to deal comprehensively with the problem, and treat victims as well as abusers.

The Police as Mediators in Family Violence: A Cautionary Note

One of the initiatives of the police force in recent years regarded the involvement of the police in mediating disputes at the community level (particularly those that have the potential for family violence). The idea is to be commended and one hopes that this programme will be continued. It is a creative idea, which has extended the concept of community policing, but we need to be very careful in implementing this proposal, as counselling a family is, under normal circumstances, a complex task requiring some amount of professional skill and a lot of experience.

In our quest for solutions to the problem of family violence, let us not rush to provide "quick-fix" solutions, which may make matters worse in the long run. Spousal abuse is seen by many policemen as family business and, therefore, when abused women appeal to them for assistance, they are resistant to interfering in what they perceive as a "normal" family squabble. All policemen need to have this matter included as part of their basic training curriculum or in-service training curriculum. If we focus on the issue of confidentiality, for example, which is based on mutual trust and respect, given the history of mistrust that has existed for decades between the police and the community, we could be in for serious trouble if our policemen are not adequately trained.

When families are violent, or have the potential for violence, experience and know-how in dealing with crisis situations is even more important. The fact is, mediation and intervention in issues related to individuals and families are tasks that should be tackled by persons with a lot more than a one- or two-day workshop in mediation. The important principle of confidentiality, and the problem of the transference of personal feelings from oneself to one's client, are just some of the issues that trained counsellors spend years perfecting, under the watchful eyes of experienced educators and practitioners, before they are expected to work with the public. The institutionalization of mediation training for the police through curriculum inputs in the police training school must therefore be made a priority, and an attempt should be made to create a cadre of specialists in this area who could be assigned to different regions upon graduation.

In a 1994 study on the perpetrators of family violence, the results showed that the largest occupational group referred to a social service agency for perpetrating family violence was found to be security officers, including soldiers, police and security guards. Putting the wrong police officers into mediation counselling, therefore, with exposure to only a few workshops will not be enough to address some of the fundamental problems in our communities and in our police force. The idea should be thought through carefully, and the programme should be guided by the following steps.

- An employee assistance programme within the police force: The police force should start with itself, and try to change attitudes and behaviour from within the force. This would involve having professionally trained staff employed by the force to deal with some of the stresses that police officers face at the individual/interpersonal level, and the family level. A newspaper report some time ago lamented the fact that a psychiatrist was no longer available to assist with counselling within the police force. There is now a well-established chaplaincy with a rural network of counsellors within the police force. Given the country's resources, it is proposed that the police force make use of these chaplains as full time counsellors, and ensure that they have training in social work or psychology. These counsellors could develop an employee assistance programme for the entire force to deal with officers who are drug abusers, alcoholics, perpetrators of family violence and those with other interpersonal problems. This kind of programme is standard practice in most big organizations in the developed world, as well as in some developing countries, and is used as a mechanism for dealing with problems employees experience within many big organizations. With such a system in place, the trained employee assistance staff person could then refer those in need of specialized care, medication or long term psychoanalysis to a psychiatrist, which would make the service more cost effective in the long term. Stress management programmes must also be instituted for every station, but especially those in difficult crime areas.
- The use of psychological testing for the police: The use of psychological testing and screening instruments, to determine those officers most suitable for deployment as mediation officers, is another practice that could be included in the recruiting process, to improve the quality of staff in the force generally, and make the mediation programme more effective.
- Expanding the cadre of specially trained police officers: The existing cadre of persons within the police force who are trained in social work, human relations, and/or basic psychology should be expanded. Once trained

these staff members could then be deployed to those sensitive areas of police work related to children and families, such as rape, child abuse, spousal abuse, etc.

- Training of trainers: This cadre of trained personnel could also act as a core group to train others in the art of community policing and human relations, strengthening initiatives with youth and children, as through police youth clubs, working with "detached youth" or youth at risk for getting in gangs and youth under the control of local community dons.
- Parish response teams: Parish response teams should be established for all family mediation, family violence, and child related issues involving the police. Each parish response team would include at least one trained officer, with allocations based on the incidence of family violence in that parish.
- Family violence, the police and child abuse management: The parish response teams for family mediation as a response to family violence could also be integrated into the proposals that have been put forward on child abuse management. The child abuse advocates in Jamaica, spearheaded by Dr Pauline Milbourne, have for years proposed the establishment of parish response teams to deal with violence against children, with one member of that team being a police officer. It is proposed that police officers be trained to deal with all violence within the family in terms of intervention strategies and techniques of mediation for child abuse as well as other forms of family violence. Once the police officers receive appropriate training, they will be able to determine which cases need referral to existing agencies for further treatment, and which cases can be handled at the community level by the mediation officers.

In conclusion, therefore, the idea of using police officers for mediation is an innovative approach to community policing, but we need to have trained officers in place who know what they are doing, and who understand how their activity relates to the broader framework of social service delivery in our society. Only then can this new initiative avoid duplication and make sense in the broader scheme of things.

Access to Children and Family Services

Given the increase in murder/suicides in recent years, another issue related to service delivery for domestic violence concerns the perception of access to services. The Children's Services Division, which has a network of agencies across the country, should be reorganized to provide preventive services for both children and families, so that couples do not resort to murder/suicide as a means of resolving their problems. It is necessary for this unit to take responsibility for family intervention. Increasingly a variety of other individuals and groups in the society are attempting to fill the void. We need to ensure that the activities of these individuals and groups are carefully monitored by professional bodies to make sure that the public receives the quality of service it deserves. Normally, family therapists are graduate level social workers or clinical psychologists who spend a considerable period after graduation doing continuing education courses in family therapy under the guidance and supervision of an accredited family therapist. The professional social workers and psychologists who work with families need to update their training and accreditation systems in this area to ensure that individuals who claim to be family therapists are in fact trained appropriately.

Legislative Matters Affecting Children: Parental Input

Domestic violence is one of Jamaica's social problems that has not been addressed seriously for some time. In order to make inroads into the prevention and management of this problem, it is important to deal with the issue systematically, allowing for the greatest possible input from social services. This issue, as well as other child and family matters needing legislative intervention, presents us with a special opportunity to broaden our democratic institutions. It is suggested that special parliamentary or community fora be held, for this and other issues affecting the child and family. It is suggested that various interest groups be given the opportunity to speak directly to parliamentarians and community leaders on different sides of the political fence, so that amendments to laws and bills can be considered formally and intelligently, in the best interest of the nation's children and families.

SEX AND CHILDREN: ARE OUR CHILDREN OVEREXPOSED?

The following is adapted from an article that was published in a weekly column in The Children's Lobby, *which was published by the Jamaica Herald on Wednesday, 16 February, 1994.*

On a trip to Ocho Rios some years ago, a family and some friends visited a popular public beach in the tourist resort area. This particular beach is one of the favourite haunts in that area, for Jamaicans and tourists alike. There were three women and one man in the family group, accompanied by four girls aged 17, 13, 10 and 3, and two boys aged 5 and 7. An otherwise unspoiled interlude of relaxation was marked by a rather pointed observation — that of bare-breasted women of all ages languishing on the sand or on beach chairs, and wading or swimming in the water. Some of these women were with male companions. All of them appeared to be tourists. None appeared to be anything but comfortably oblivious to all, except for the sand, sea, sun and the occasional casual conversation with one of the number of Jamaican men who either work or hustle on the beach. There was one couple who remained locked in a passionate embrace, in about three feet of water, and in full view of anyone on that stretch of the beach. That strip of beach is surrounded by hotel properties that cater to families – hotels whose patrons were given access to the beach as a part of their vacation privileges. The reality was that this family beach was dotted with bare-breasted women from Europe and North America, and, in Jamaica in 1995 no one seemed to be concerned except for the parents in this family group who were at their wits end trying to explain to their elementary school aged youngsters what was happening.

The Free Market

This happens in Jamaica one assumes because of the free market system which guides the marketing of our tourism product. What is the message entrenched in the guiding philosophy? Anything goes, as long as money is being made; illegality may be dallied with, just don't get caught; moral suasion springs, not from conscience, but from the balance sheet, and the bottom line is the ultimate arbiter of right or wrong. If it is good for business (translated "right"), then too bad if it may not be good for you, your children or your neighbour's grandchildren! The messages that are being disseminated, and the ways in which the underlying meanings are transmitted and received, are significant in the context of our concern for how we raise our children and how our society reinforces or erodes what we teach them.

Confusing Messages to Our Children

The above discussion suggests that there is a common thread associated with certain aspects of Jamaican life that is sending messages of dubious merit to our children. This thread is being woven into a fabric of disrespect for moral authority in favour of engendering support for and increasing the momentum of "popular" sentiment which glorifies that which is raucous, uncouth, or even misguidedly "progressive." What appears to validate this sentiment is the fact that huge dollar signs are plastered over the garments and other trappings of a sufficient number of those who would wear this fabric, some of whom hold positions of "respectability" in our society. Not to forget those who would embrace this type of behaviour as part of an emerging "cultural expression." Common decency therefore becomes increasingly uncommon. One would not want to advocate either the extremely puritanical paradigms of the past or the excesses of so-called liberalism evident in the more developed quarters of the global village. The much touted global village is spreading, and with it, both the good and the not-so-good.

Raising our Children in the Global Village

It is becoming increasingly difficult to raise our children with the sense of identity and the value systems that we would wish to inculcate in them, partly because we allow our society to indiscriminately absorb external influences, without any apparent will to filter out what would otherwise be morally infectious or objectionable, partly because big dollars run behind these trends. Observe the trend in foreign music videos, internet entertainment and the readily visible adaptations of these trends by local artistes, many of whom are in fact based in North America. We must expose our children in order to educate them but we must protect and supervise them continuously.

Creativity and Entrepreneurship vs. Social Disintegration

Observe the scene on a "family" resort beach. Listen to the offensive but nevertheless popular lyrics of many musical selections played on radio, or blaring from powerful sound systems in many of our communities on any day or night, often until the early morning hours, or in our buses and taxis during the day. There are many other examples of our children being over exposed to trends that are disturbingly on the rise, setting newer "norms" that are already tugging at the social fabric of our beloved country, "norms" that may yet rip this fabric apart.

One acknowledges that there is a tremendous pool of creativity in this nation, both in business and cultural expression. One further acknowledges that this is, potentially and in reality, one of our most valuable assets as a people. But we have to be careful that creativity in business or in cultural expression is not guided solely by flashing the dollar sign, to the extent that this spawns socially destructive patterns that tear down the values and attitudes that we are trying so hard to inculcate in our children. Let us not allow the decisions concerning nudity on our family beaches (like other decisions regarding sexually explicit lyrics etc.) to fall too far to the bottom line! (No pun intended.)

CHILDREN AND THE MEDIA

As we are all aware, Jamaican culture and fashion, as well as what we eat, what we buy, and how we behave are heavily influenced by European and North American trends. This has had benefits in terms of the positive aspects of those societies which we have adopted, such as democracy and a basic social infrastructure, but we have also received the negative repercussions in the form of drug abuse, an emphasis on materialism, etc. One of the cultural phenomena of the United States, to which we seem attracted, is the "new breed" of talk shows, made popular by media magnate Oprah Winfrey, which one could refer to as "the Oprah syndrome". (The "Oprah syndrome" may be defined for the purposes of this discussion as the mechanism by which attempts are made to analyze and solve personal problems of individuals, groups, or families on national television.) Usually this is done by using a team of "quick-fix" experts who are expected to provide solutions on the spot.

Television Coverage of Victims of Rape and Other Sexual Violence

A few years ago, a local television station aired an interview with an adolescent girl who had suffered the very traumatic experience of being gang-raped. Such an experience can lead to a variety of mental disorders, ranging from post-traumatic stress disorder, depression and mood disorders, to a possible psychotic disorder in later years. The ability of the victim to recover from such an experience is dependent to a large extent on the support that he or she receives immediately following the incident, as well as how the victim's problem is managed by the different agencies and social service personnel with which he or she may come into contact, in reporting and dealing with the incident.

The role of the media in dealing with these sensitive personal issues is, therefore, of utmost importance, as a few ill-chosen words from an inexperienced interviewer can have a damaging effect on the psychological health of the victim. One has the impression that sensationalism, as dictated by this so-called "Oprah syndrome", has been prompting our young media workers in particular to infringe on the rights of victims in some situations, particularly children. Oprah Winfrey is a professional. Many of our young media workers are at risk of losing their sense of professionalism in this regard.

Protocol for Dealing with Victims of Sexual Violence

The fact is, there is a wrong way and a right way to interview rape victims and other victims of sexual violence. If these victims are children, the matter is even more sensitive. Asking extremely personal questions of the victim on national television, shortly after the incident, is not the way those matters should be handled, if we are conducting our affairs in the best interest of the child. Media personnel must be helped by social service personnel to follow a written protocol of behaviour regarding the management of the victims of sexual violence.

Training for Media Personnel

If this is not already done, media personnel should receive basic training in normal and abnormal psychology. They should at least be trained to be sensitive to these issues. No matter how sensational it may seem to the media house, a child who is having difficulty coping psychologically with such an experience is not a good candidate for a nationally broadcast television interview. This incident therefore, highlights the tremendous responsibilities that media houses face in dealing with some of the more sensitive social issues that they must report on. When these incidents concern children, we must be even more careful, as practitioners in other countries have found that the glare of publicity regarding a sexually abusive incident, for example, can be even more traumatic than the incident itself.

In fact, the treatment plan developed for the management of sexual abuse cases in some other countries now stipulates that the victim be interviewed by only one trained professional. This means that police officers, medical practitioners, school social workers and court officers would have access to the report done by a trained intake worker at the agency of contact. This is done primarily to protect the victim.

Codes of Conduct for the Media

Policies like this can only be beneficial to potential victims and their families. Let us adopt some of the child protective policies of our neighbours to the north, and reject the negative aspects of their media, which tends to glorify and sensationalize what are very personal issues. Let us not follow willy-nilly into the footsteps of the foreign press in this regard, a foreign press which is being severely criticized by its own society. Let us be careful to adhere to our own media codes of conduct on these and other matters.

Children's Media Watch Needed!

Over the past few years, there has been growing concern about the proliferation of popular music that is laced with lewd sexual innuendos and coarse, sometimes vulgar, references to parts of the male and female anatomy. Given the fact that this is occurring in a media climate where television exposes children to extreme forms of violence, both in their news coverage, (where even infants and toddlers are exposed to corpses and mutilated bodies on a regular basis), and in their entertainment programming, there seems to be a national campaign to expose children to as much violence and as much adult sexual imagery as possible. It would be pertinent to suggest that the Jamaican media seems not at all child friendly!

A few years ago a decision was taken by one media house to "bump" TLC (The Learning Channel) to bring us every detail of the trial of an American athlete accused of killing his wife. There was little thought to the fact that there is a dearth of good educational programmes for children in Jamaica, and that many preschoolers and the kindergarten crowd look forward to that time of day to learn and have fun. The Sesame Street slot was at the time the only period of the day allotted for children on our national television stations. One assumed that the "OJ mania" that occurred in the United States did require some kind of media response here in the Caribbean, but the media here needed to also remember that the American or Canadian kindergartner has a much wider range of options for learning via television on any given afternoon. This is just a simple example, but it is used to illustrate the fact that our media planners need to be much more sensitive to the special needs of our children when preparing their programme schedules, given the reality that wholesome family entertainment in both rural and urban Jamaica is difficult to come by for most families. How can the media assist parents and families with this ongoing problem? We suggest that the Press Association of Jamaica and the Caribbean media in general, consider the issue of the development of local children's programmes and give serious thought to its very important role in the shaping of the intellect and direction of young minds. There are a number of suggestions as to how one could begin to look at this issue.

When one considers local productions such as the National Pantomime, we all agree that the annual productions are usually excellent fare for both children and adults, but especially for children. Many children who see the shows keep singing the songs and are usually still talking about the production weeks after seeing it. Parents and children would like to be able to access this material on video cassettes for home use. Pantomime productions would make a wonderful local sing-along collection for any Jamaican family.

- Is it possible that some test marketing could be done by 'weaving' sections of shows such as the Pantomime (or ASHE's performances, for example) into local children's programming?
- Could there be some focus on the development of specialists in the area of children's programming using the resources of the Caribbean Institute of Media and Communication (CARIMAC) of the University of the West Indies and The Edna Manley School for the Performing Arts? It appears that there may not be enough trained professionals in this area.

Given the large pool of creative talent available in our country, professional theatre may be ignoring the children's market to the detriment of the next generations. Using resources such as the National Pantomine, ASHE and the Catherine Levy players, the local media could produce much material that can be fed into local children's programming to strengthen it and give it some regional character.

More programmes need to be developed by children for children, in which they are given a voice to speak out on matters affecting them on a daily basis. The Jamaica Coalition on the Rights of the Child has found, in their youth fora across the country, that children are eager and able to express themselves very articulately on matters affecting them, such as transportation, child abuse, the rights of children, the constitution, etc. The media could exploit this further by placing bites of children's commentary into local children's programmes.

Is it possible that by providing greater opportunities for our children to express themselves, through programming decisions that are more sensitive to their needs, by being less willing to publicize and glorify violence and blatant sexuality in the content of media programmes, we could be instrumental in preventing some of the chaos we are now seeing in families and communities across this country?

Parent's Resource Kit

The information in the following section is presented in a format that allows individual topics to be removed for use by Parent Teachers Associations and other community based parent groups.

Parenting skills are learned,
We are not born with them,
We have to care how we grow them.
VOUCH 1986

Parenting After Divorce

Like in most other countries, the average Jamaican family structure has changed somewhat over the last quarter of a century. More women are in the labor force than there were 25 years ago, and there are also more single parent families today than there were at that time, many of these families being headed by women. One factor (not often discussed in the sociological literature) that has given rise to the increase in the number of single-parent households with female heads and other types of nontraditional families, such as blended families, is the increase in the number of divorced and separated families in Jamaica.

One of the problems that is often of concern to divorced parents is how to ensure that the quality of parenting continues and is unimpaired after the separation of the parents.

Here are some possible suggestions for parents:

* Both parents, singly or together, should spend time with the child on a regular basis, before, during, and after divorce proceedings in order to explain what is happening in the family and why it is happening, and what is going to happen.

- Parents should repeatedly reinforce the fact that the divorce and/or separation is not the child's fault and that both parents still love him or her very much.
- Let the child know that you understand how painful the experience will be for him or her. Let him or her know that you also experience pain and that you will be there to help him or her through the difficult times. Anticipate the difficult times, and do not hesitate to go for counselling with your child when these times confront you.
- Try not to speak critically or negatively about an ex-spouse in the presence of the child. Never use the child as a "weapon" against an ex-spouse. Though it is tempting, this activity will damage your child emotionally in the long term.
- Once parents have separated and live in two different households, parents should try to work out visitation and custody arrangements that are in the child's best interest. Parents should also agree on child rearing practices, which are in the best interests of the child. (Remember children need consistency and stability. Different rules in two households can add to their confusion and can result in rebellion and other acting out behaviour.)
- Parents should not try to compensate for their absence/loss by being overly indulgent towards the child.
- Both parents must realize and accept that *parenthood does not end with divorce* and often both parents have to work harder at parenting than before. *Parenthood is the one link that binds ex-spouses for life.*

How To Help The Sensitive Child

Children are born with a wide variety of temperaments. Psychologists and researchers in the area of child development have found that at birth, and even prior to birth, the child's basic nature is well defined. This is due to the fact that "temperament" is determined from genetic influences, and therefore a child's degree of sensitivity or lack of it, comes partly from the personalities of both his parents.

One of the major concerns of parents is how to help the child who is sensitive, who does not make friends easily, or is easily hurt by others. In an attempt to deal with this problem, parents may get angry at the child, and try to force a change in his/her behaviour. They may wring their hands in despair, wishing that their child could be more resilient, and they may resort to over protectiveness. Much of this behavior comes from a fear, on the part of parents, that their child will be unable to cope later with life's many problems.

WHAT SHOULD PARENTS DO?

* Do accept the fact that your child is a unique individual with his or her own strengths and weaknesses. *Children need to know that they are cherished and loved for themselves.*
* Do help your child to gradually develop the strengths to deal with specific problems.
* Do keep close to your child and talk with him or her on a daily basis. Set aside a little quiet time each day to discuss the day's events and help sort out worrying events.
* Do help your child to enjoy life and develop a sense of humour. Plan frequent family activities where your child can relax and enjoy life's simple pleasures, for example nature walks, talking together, going to the supermarket together, playing board games and card games.

What Should Parents Not Do?

* Do not ever compare your child to other children, such as their neighbours, classmates and peers.
* Do not criticize or ridicule him or her for being different.
* Never pressure your child to be the best all the time, for example at dancing, football, art, ballet. Allow your child to find his or her own level.
* Do not encourage your child to "take life too seriously", and worry over every hurt or unpleasant event.

You can bring out what is best in your child by positively reinforcing and building on what is already there, rather than trying to make him or her into someone he or she may never be.

3

Punishment And Discipline: Tools Or Weapons?

The twin issues of the punishment and discipline of children have probably been controversial issues in the area of child rearing ever since civilization began. Historically, the idea that children are individuals, with their own rights and minds of their own, is a relatively recent assumption in child rearing practice. For centuries, children were seen as miniature adults, having no special needs or emotions that were different from those of adults. The correct way to bring up children at that time, therefore, was to ensure that the evil that was supposedly inherent in a child's make up was eliminated, and so children were often punished harshly, physically and emotionally. Child abuse at the societal level was rampant, and child labour was commonplace.

Today in most modern societies, we pride ourselves on the fact that we no longer rear our children in this manner. Children are seen as blessed, and having a special and privileged position in society. In Caribbean society, though we all hold this view, the issues of discipline and punishment still generate some degree of confusion in the minds of some parents and care givers. Very often, parents and care givers wonder how little or how much punishment to use, or when to use discipline and when not to. The result is that child rearing styles in most Caribbean societies today range from family situations where children are physically and emotionally abused, to families where no discipline is used at all. Often there is much focus and media attention on the former scenario, due to the obvious damage that is done to the child and to the family's functioning, but the child who receives little or no discipline may become similarly impaired in terms of his or her potential for functioning socially.

Unfortunately, many parents think that loving our children means making excuses for their misbehaviour. We accept and rationalize much inappropriate behaviour in the home, in the school, and in the community. Jamaican parents who have recently become socially mobile become slaves to their children, providing them with every conceivable luxury in the belief that these luxuries make them good parents. However, cellular phones, cable television, and expensive toys are no substitutes for loving parents who insist on the same discipline of mind and body that their grandparents did. Many children move from childhood through adolescence, to adulthood, without clear guidelines and rules of conduct, and are therefore unable to conform to the social norms of their community and, ultimately, their society.

What Is Discipline and How Can it Be Used?

Unfortunately discipline is often thought to be synonymous with the physical abuse of children. In reality, discipline refers to the process by which one trains or develops a child's sense of wrong and right by instruction. It could also be seen as a mechanism for instilling order. Through discipline a child may be taught self control. Parents have the responsibility to help the child to do this relatively complex task. Discipline can therefore be seen as a tool that parents can use to achieve some kind of order in the life of the child, through a well thought out set of guidelines and rules of behaviour.

Children need some structure, and they need clear boundaries for behaviour. Leaving a child to work out his own boundaries means leaving him to flounder by himself in a world of disorder and chaos. This can be very confusing to a child.

What Should Parents Do?

When trying to work out a system of discipline for your child remember the following:

* Try not to let disciplinary issues become power struggles between child and parent. Involve your child in the disciplinary process.
* The needs of your child change at every stage of his development. Try to find out as much as you can about your child's development and what to expect at each stage. Try to ensure that punishment is age appropriate, and is appropriate to the child's need.
* Try using positive reinforcement as much as possible in rewarding children.
* Make use of the family unit when possible to resolve conflict situations.
* Try not to start discipline during adolescence. Discipline in its simplest form starts in the early years of childhood.

More useful information can be obtained from the videotape entitled *Discipline and Punishment for the Jamaican Child* (listed in the Resource Material section of this chapter).

Child Abuse And Neglect

Incidence and Characteristics

The full extent of child abuse and neglect in Jamaica is not known accurately. This is due partly to the fact that many cases of child abuse and neglect go unreported, as the reporting of child abuse is not mandatory by law. However, preliminary data from the Child Guidance Clinic in 1996 reported *over 6,000 cases* of child abuse and neglect nationally.

The laws that govern child abuse and neglect in Jamaica state:

> Every person who having attained the age of 17 years and having the custody, charge or care of, or responsibility for any juvenile person under 17 who willfully assaults, ill-treats, neglects, abandons or exposes such juvenile, or causes or procures him to be assaulted, ill-treated, neglected, abandoned or exposed in a manner likely to cause that juvenile unnecessary suffering or injury to health (including injury to or loss of sight or hearing or limb, or organ of the body, or mental derangement) shall be guilty of a misdemeanour.

A person responsible for a child's welfare includes the child's parents, guardians, foster parents, an employee of a public or private residential home, nursery or day care centre or any other person legally responsible for the child's welfare.

Types of Child Abuse Found in Jamaica

One 1986 report on child abuse and neglect in Jamaica (Crawford-Brown 1986) reports that the most common forms of child abuse and neglect found in Jamaica are:

Physical abuse: Examples of physical abuse include shaking, beating, burning, hitting with a belt, stick, or hose.

Emotional abuse: This may involve the failure to provide a loving environment or adequate care and supervision for the child. It may also involve the care-giver ignoring or rejecting the child. Emotional abuse includes verbal abuse, in which the care-giver belittles, yells at or criticizes the child constantly, and threatens the child.

Sexual abuse: Any form of sexual activity between an adult and child where the adult gains sexual gratification from the activity. This may involve fondling and may or may not involve penile penetration. It is important to note that this act is defined as sexual abuse whether or not the child experiences pleasure as a result of the activity.

Institutional abuse: This involves endangering a child's physical, social, or psychological welfare. It includes action perpetrated by an institution, or a staff member at the institution, or by the social welfare system against a child or a group of children. Institutions include schools, courts, children's homes, or other child care institutions, foster homes, health, welfare, or other social service delivery systems.

Physical neglect: This is the denial of a child's right to have his or her physical needs met and may involve the failure to provide food, clothing or shelter. Physical neglect may also involve willful neglect or blatant rejection, as in the case of abandonment. Abandonment can be described as the most extreme form of neglect.

Medical neglect: This is the wilful denial of a child's right to receive medical attention when needed. It may involve refusal by a care-giver to take a child for immunization or medical attention, for example when the care-giver is aware of the need for such medical attention and when such medical attention is available.

Educational neglect: This is the denial of a child's right to be exposed to a consistent educational environment. (It is important to note that factors associated with poverty must be ruled out in coming to a determination of each of these forms of neglect.)

Common Signs of Child Abuse and Neglect

The **physically abused child** may have cuts, abrasions (scrapes), bruises, welts, sores, scars, head injuries, broken bones (such as broken ribs) and other signs of harsh beatings. The **sexually abused child** can be a girl or a boy who may have a discharge from, and/or bruises, to the genital or anal area. He or she may also have a venereal disease (VD). Such a child is at risk for contracting AIDS or other sexually transmitted diseases. The **emotionally abused child** may be very aggressive, unnaturally quiet or timid, or may be extremely shy. Such a child may have learning problems or may develop more slowly than most children of his or her age group.

Some other signs of child abuse are poor attendance at school, aggression, hyperactivity, little capacity for joy (a characteristic which may be lifelong), shyness, poor self concept, wariness of physical contact, and a decrease in academic performance. A sexually abused child may become promiscuous or have difficulty in dealing with sexual intimacy in later life or may become clinically depressed or manifest other serious psychological problems. The **neglected child** could be abandoned, appear malnourished, exhibit a vacant stare, may have frequent illnesses and is usually left alone to wander and beg. It is important to state that some children with strong family and other support may show no major abnormal symptoms.

Suicidal Ideation

Children who are abused or neglected, as well as other categories of emotionally disturbed children, may present withdrawn or depressive behaviour, which may or may not include suicidal ideation. This involves the child frequently expressing a desire to end his or her life. This may be expressed to peers, teachers or significant others. It may also involve drawing pictures that depict the end of the child's life; for example, drawings of coffins or tombstones with his or her name depicted graphically. Children who are sexually and/or emotionally abused or neglected for prolonged periods are at particular risk for the development of suicidal ideation. Such children should be referred to a trained health care or allied professional immediately, for example a psychiatrist, clinical psychologist, or clinical social worker. It is important to note that these characteristics may also be symptomatic of a depressive illness, drug abuse or other psychological problem, so it is important for children and adolescents to be referred to an experienced professional in order that an assessment can be done at an early stage.

Major Characteristics of Adolescent Suicidal Behaviour

It is important that guidance counsellors be made aware of the major characteristics of adolescent suicidal behaviour so that these cases can be referred to the appropriate personnel immediately. These characteristics are as follows:

- Adolescents who attempt suicide often do not think that they will die and attempt the act of suicide in order to bring attention to their problems. Their attempts to draw attention to themselves and their problems should not be ignored.
- Adolescents will consistently express a desire to end their lives. They will express this to friends, teachers and other adults whom they trust,

and sometimes parents. Every statement expressing suicidal ideation should be taken seriously until an appropriate professional is satisfied that the behaviour can be attributed to some other factor.

* Adolescents who suddenly withdraw from peer-related activities may also be at risk for suicide, and parents should bring this to the attention of a professional quickly.
* Adolescents who are at risk for suicide may exhibit a sudden or unexplained "gift-giving" of prized possessions.

It is important to note that these stages and behaviours are guidelines and do not always indicate childhood or adolescent suicide or child abuse for that matter. Any child manifesting **one or more** of these signs should be reported to the agencies and professionals mentioned at the end of this chapter.

The treatment of child abuse is a complex process and should be left to a trained person. The identification of the symptoms of child abuse by relatives is a straightforward one, so community persons such as health aides, and street animators who have received some basic training in child abuse and neglect detection can do basic identification of this problem at the community level. Once detected, however, community persons should not hesitate to refer these cases to the relevant agency nearest to their community for follow up assessment and possible treatment.

Where Does Child Abuse Happen and Who Abuses?

Child abuse occurs in middle class, upper middle class, as well as poor households. Child abuse may occur in rural or urban areas, in schools or other institutions for children. Any parent, guardian, or other family member has the potential to abuse a child. It is important to note that any of these family members can learn to reduce the tendency to abuse their child. Consequently, *child welfare practices must be adjusted to include rehabilitation of parents or guardians as well as children.*

Treating the Family

Identification and treatment of entire families is very important, as abused children in turn often grow up to be abusers themselves. Unfortunately too may of our child and family agencies work with the child by himself or herself and the family is often neglected, ensuring that the abuse will continue. Treating the child is an important aspect of dealing with child abuse but this must always be done in consultation with parents. One innovation that could prove useful in the juvenile justice system in Jamaica is the 'sentencing of parents' to periods of treatment along with their children. The notion of 'plucking' children out of their families and sentencing them to a fit person order in a nontherapeutic children's institution is as backward as it is nonproductive. Parental and family involvement in treating child abuse must be the direction we take as we move into the twenty-first century.

Why Do Parents Abuse Their Children?

Some reasons are:

- They suffered abuse/mistreatment as children
- Lack of parenting knowledge
- Expecting too much from children, and not understanding the developmental stages and needs of children
- Financial problems and unemployment, which create frustration and stress, which are then transmitted to the child
- Insecurity and immaturity, particularly among teenaged parents
- Alcohol or drug problems, or other forms of addiction, such as gambling
- Inability to manage children single handedly, for example, single parents

Which Children Are More at Risk for Abuse or Neglect?

- Children who are unwanted, for example those born as a result of rape, and children born to teenaged mothers;
- Children who are difficult to manage for behavioural or physical reasons, such as hyperactive children, children with attention deficit disorder, or those who have learning problems, children who are mentally or physically handicapped, as well as children who have chronic illnesses such as asthma, sickle cell disease, or children who have AIDS;
- Children who are a constant reminder of unpleasant, traumatic experiences or those who physically resemble someone who brings back unpleasant memories, for example an absent father or mother.

Who Are Abused Children?

A few examples are:

- Children who are repeatedly ignored, belittled, embarrassed or accused of being slow, stupid or "dunce";

- Children who are repeatedly called "black and ugly" or called worthless, for example for not gaining a place in high school, or as a result of failing the Common Entrance, CXC or other examination;
- Children who are shaken, pushed, pinched, tied up, beaten with electric cords or ill treated in any way (beating a child for stealing or for not learning as fast as other children does not solve the problem: the child only becomes aggressive and defiant towards others);
- Children who are left unprotected or with elderly grandparents or friends who cannot adequately care for them or love them, or children left by parents who migrate to other countries without providing adequate alternative care; children whose parents migrate may receive material gifts, but often lack the emotional nurturing to enhance their social and emotional development;
- Children who are burnt with cigarettes, irons, hot coals, or scalded with hot water or beaten mercilessly with branches from the nearest tree;
- Children who are prevented from attending school in order to take care of their younger brothers and sisters;
- Children who are separated from their parents too often and passed from relative to relative or from friend to friend, or who change guardians too often to develop a close relationship with a parent figure;
- Children whose mothers, fathers, stepfathers, other relatives or strangers have sexual intercourse with them, fondle them, or expose them to adult activity via computers, videos, adult magazines or other reading material;
- Children in institutions who are teased about the circumstances of their family background or children who are "taken advantage of" by staff members of children's homes or correctional institutions;
- Children who are pushed off buses, or who are fondled while they are passengers on a crowded bus.

Children who present with one or more of the above problems and who express these as problems should be referred to the nearest agency providing services to children.

SUMMARY

Most of the issues raised in this chapter had specific recommendations presented in summary form for use by parents. The sections that focused on parenting addressed the attempts made by some parents to provide children with some of the material things which they never had. The chapter discussed the fact that children are often showered with inappropriate visual images through the electronic media via cable television, video tapes and other programming and pointed to methods that parents can use to monitor this exposure. It was recommended that parents should never relinquish their parental responsibilities and should hold fast to time-tested traditional values and morals, using these to guide them in child rearing practice, despite media and other influences to the contrary.

Measures suggested for addressing these issues included the following:

- Monitoring all in-coming information to your child from printed material and the electronic media, to ensure that their content is appropriate to the level of development and maturity of your child.
- Keeping all sexually explicit adult material (books, magazines, videos, etc.) safely locked away and out of the reach of children and adolescents. This includes any Internet access that provides exposure to pornographic material.
- Involving yourself intimately and talking with your children about their activities on a regular basis. Parents must try to hear what their children are saying and to whom they are talking.
- Use of community based strategies, through the mass media, focused on parenting education to ensure that remedial information is made available to parents. Community based groups, such as Parenting Partners and the Coalition For Better Parenting, are possible resources in this area of concern.

There is much that is unique in our society about our attitudes to parenting, and we need to deal with these issues and set a standard for parenting education, which can guide trainers throughout the country and in fact, throughout the Caribbean. Publication of local parenting material through books, videotapes and manuals provides us with a model that should be explored by educational and other institutions developed to help parents. The media can play a tremendous role in helping to disseminate this information.

RESOURCE MATERIAL

Books and Documents

Dinkmeyer, D. and McKay, D. 1989. *The Parent Handbook*. Pines, MN: American Guidance Service.

Dodson, E. 1987. *How to Single Parent*. New York: Harper & Row.

Elmers, R. and Hutchinson, R. 1977. *Effective Parents, Responsible Children*. New York: McGraw-Hill.

Gillgorell, B. 1984. *Working with Families*. London: MacMillan.

Goldstein, S. 1987. *Divorced Parenting: How to Make it Work*. London: Cedars Publishers.

Knight, B.M. 1980. *Enjoying Single Parenthood*. New York: Van Nostrand Reinhold.

Krielkamp, T. 1989. *Time-Limited Intermittent Therapy with Children and Families*. New York: Brunner/Mazel.

Maddox, B. 1975. *The Half-Parent: Living with Other People's Children*. London: Ebenezer Baylus & Sons.

Parenting Partners Inc. 1996. *Pathways to Parenting (A Comprehensive Manual for Trainers)*. Kingston, Jamaica.

Pearce, J. 1989. *Fighting, Teasing and Bullying*. London: Thorsons Publishers.

Trasler, G. 1989. *In Place of Parents*. London: Routledge & Kegan Paul.

Wilmes, D. 1988. *Parenting for Prevention*. Minneapolis: Thorsons Publishers.

Wood, K. 1986. *Family and Delinquency*. New York: Human Sciences Press.

Wood, K. and Geismar, L. 1989. *Families at Risk: Treating the Multi Problem Family*. New York: Family Press.

Books/Tools for Working with Children and Parents

Boulden, J. and Boulden, J. 1992. *Secrets that Hurt, Sexual Abuse Activity Book*. New York: Golden Press.

Blake, F. *Why Is my Family Different? (A Book About Blended Families)*. New York: Golden Press.

Ernest, K.E. 1993. *Hope Leaves Jamaica*. London: Methuen Children's Books.

Child Guidance Clinic, Ministry of Health. 1989. *A Story About Me* (A Colouring Book for Abused Children). Kingston, Jamaica.

Child Guidance Clinic, Ministry of Health - Pamphlet Series. 1994. *Child Sexual Abuse, Physical Abuse of Children*. Kingston, Jamaica.

Voluntary Organization for the Upliftment of Children. 1987. *Facts on Child Abuse*. Pamphlet. Kingston, Jamaica: Committee on Child Abuse and Neglect.

Audiovisual Material

* 3-D Projects, *Parent-to-Parent Counselling: A Guide for Assisting Parents of Children with Disabilities* (videotape and manual). St Catherine, Jamaica: Pear Tree Press.

** Cerfe, S. 1993. *Discipline and Punishment for the Jamaican Child* (an instructional videotape). Kingston, Jamaica: University of the West Indies, Department of Sociology and Social Work/Caribbean Institute for Media and Communications (CARIMAC).

** Caribbean Media Services. 1995. *Child Sexual Abuse in Jamaica* (a videotape for parents). Kingston, Jamaica: Caribbean Child Development Centre.

Referral Sources and Agency Contacts

Parenting Partners
c/o British Save the Children Fund
National Heroes Circle
Kingston 4

Coalition for Better Parenting
c/o Ministry of Education,
Youth and Culture
National Heroes Circle
Kingston 4

Help for Parents (a direct
service agency)
1a Trevennion Park Road
Kingston 5

Fathers Incorporated
56 Old Hope Road
Kingston 5

*   This videotape is available for
purchase through 3-D Projects, 14 Monk
Street, Spanish Town P.O., St. Catherine.

**   These videotapes are available for
rental through the Children's Lobby,
c/o Mico Youth Counselling Centre. A
security deposit is required on all tapes
rented.

5

The Jamaican Child of the Nineties

INTRODUCTION

The 1990s has been a difficult decade for children in Jamaica. The number of children and youth on the streets, aged 0-17 years, estimated to be 50 in 1980, was estimated to be 2,500 by 1991 (UNICEF 1996). That report estimated working children in Jamaica to number 23,000, and the number of children actually living on the streets was estimated to be between 2,000 to 2,500. Children and youth reported as being out of school in Jamaica numbered 13,000 as of July 1995 (Planning Institute of Jamaica 1995c). Children in need of care and protection, in 1994, as evidenced by the number of child care and protection cases before the Family Courts in Kingston and Montego Bay, numbered approximately 1,276. Children with disabilities were estimated at approximately 82,000 in 1996 and children in institutions (child care only) numbered over 2,000 (Planning Institute of Jamaica 1995c). Cases of abused and neglected children and youth, as recorded by the Child Abuse and Neglect Registry in 1995, totalled 3,500 cases that were referred over a two year period.

The actual number of children who are abused and neglected in Jamaica is still not known. In the latest "Situation Analysis of Women and Children in Jamaica" report (1995), 567 children under the age of 16 years were raped in 1993. This figure represents 50 percent of the total reported incidents of rape and carnal abuse nationally. It is important to note that the average age of children raped was 9 years. The average age of these victims tends to be a bit lower than the average age in other countries. For example, the average age in the United Kingdom in 1988 was 11-13 years (Kelly 1995). As in other countries, the majority of offenders were males. In the latest "Situation Analysis of Women and Children" 1995 report, 60 percent were known to the children.

One interesting finding related to physical abuse is that children who were physically abused had a family background in which there were at least two changes in parenting figures between ages 0 and 10 years. In addition, between 1990 and 1995, the number of children dying as a result of accidents (many involving lack of supervision and neglect) increased by 50 percent over the preceding five year period.[1] These accidents included road accidents and household accidents. A significant number of these household accidents involved children being burnt by fires. As of December 1994, the number of children under 18 years with AIDS was estimated at 537.

These figures represent only a small number of the children affected as, to date, the coordination of data collecting and research capabilities on issues related to the welfare of children remains underdeveloped. These figures, however, also indicate that there are a number of issues facing our children that need urgent attention. The development of programmes and policies to meet our children's needs has not kept pace with changes in the Jamaican society. The programmes are also not structured to ensure that the rights of children are respected, and their special place in all our lives is secured. The following discussions point to some of the issues that have been highlighted as the more serious ones affecting children in our society in the last decade.

POLICY RESEARCH EVALUATION AND LINK TO PROGRAMME PLANNING

Additional research needs to be done to determine the focal points of new policies and to refine existing ones. A coherent long term strategy should be based on clear objectives to be accomplished in order to affect the quality of delivery of child care services. This will have to be done in a progressive manner, given our limited resources, building on an empirical foundation, until we create a permanent structure of high quality child care services. This will require the establishment of a unit within the existing Children's Services Division that is mandated to do research, training and evaluation, which could then be channeled into programme planning and policy development.

THE ROLE OF THE TRANSPORTATION SYSTEM IN PROMOTING VIOLENCE

If one looks at the transportation system over the decade, we remember with horror, incidents of children being literally pushed out of moving minibuses, and left to hang out of doorways to the buses on occasion. Teenage girls have been fondled and sexually molested by older adolescent and adult males when they use this mode of transportation on their way to school. The current transportation system provided for the Kingston Metropolitan area is by its very nature a violent one. The system allows careless and reckless driving. It allows its drivers to drink alcohol openly. It permits badly maintained buses in its system, many of them blaring loud and lewd music as part of the normal mode of operation These buses weave and careen dangerously through lines of traffic with adults and children hanging through their open doors as if such driving activities are a totally normal aspect of their operational practice. This is an unacceptable way to transport children and adults, to say the least. Our present transportation system is absolutely and totally unacceptable. We are transporting individuals in conditions similar to those in which our forefathers were transported across the infamous Middle Passage. The fact that the new school buses were incorporated into the old system of transportation spoilt any chance of showing our children how a civilized bus system should operate. The present system has only served to socialize our children to see anarchy, violence and antisocial behaviour as a normal way of life. Children have been mown down on roads, they have been burnt to death in their beds, as their mothers entertain themselves elsewhere. We blamed the mothers as irresponsible but do not see that as a society we have a responsibility to educate parents on an ongoing basis and to put legislation in place, so that parents, and the public generally, realize the importance of supervision and the responsibilities associated with parenting.

Styrofoam Bicycle Helmets

Many of our small children receive bicycle or motorcycle rides to school from dads or other male relatives. Sometimes two or three children are carried on one bicycle. We must not wait for a tragedy to happen before we put legislation in place to protect our little ones. Our Child Protection Act must be structured so that our laws can be enforced. We may have to consider including public education about the dangers of riding in cars without seat belts, and riding bicycles without helmets. We may have to consider, in addition, subsidizing bicycle helmets for children or issuing styrofoam helmets through our schools as part of a comprehensive prevention programme. Starting safety prevention with school aged children is one of the ways in which we can begin to develop a culture of prevention in our adult population, particularly with regard to the loss of life and limb, which is such a serious public health problem in our society.

Safety Packet Distribution in Primary Schools and Health Centres

Another innovation that would help to disseminate safety information to large numbers of families would be to distribute safety packets containing basic safety tips for parents to mothers in antenatal and "well-baby" clinics, and to children in primary, all-age, preparatory and infant schools throughout the island. If this information is made attractive and if it makes use of bold graphics and is presented in a format for easy reading, we could pass on comprehensive safety information covering all areas of child safety, including road and traffic safety as well as safety in the home. This would require a collaborative effort of medical and social practitioners, and is another way an integrated team approach can be used to solve a problem that has been affecting our children for far too long.

Road Accidents and Our Children: Parent Power

The increasing numbers of family members who have lost loved ones, particularly children, to crime and road accidents is a serious problem. Police data indicate that 400 children lost their lives over the three years prior to January 1997. These parents should be a force to be reckoned with if they could use their power to first of all influence policy regarding child safety and also to sensitize and educate the public. If by so doing we could prevent one more life being lost, it would be worth the effort.

TIME TO STAND UP FOR OUR CHILDREN

"But you do not have a life, you are only a little girl." In a conversation held one early January between a precocious 11 year old and her equally precocious three year old brother, the 11 year old said, "I have to get my life more organized this year." The three year old's response was, "But you don't have a life, you are not a wife; you don't have children, you are a little girl!" In reflecting on these statements some time later, I realized that Jamaican society (like this three year old), is also of the view that children somehow don't have lives because they are little girls and little boys. As adult members of the society many of us act as if they are really not that important to our lives. After almost 20 years of advocating for the welfare of Jamaican children (at the community level, at the level of service delivery, and at the policy level) one finds time and time again that this society pays lip service to the rights of children. We say we love our children, but if we are honest with ourselves, and look across the hills and valleys of this nation, in every district of rural Jamaica, as well as the town houses and "palaces" of uptown Kingston, Montego Bay and Mandeville, our children and families are in serious trouble. We all know this, we talk about it every day, but apart from putting a little Band-aid here and there, as a society we are not dealing with the problems of our children in a systematic and organized way.

'Criss' and Clean on the Outside

Most of our children look healthy and 'criss' on the outside. They wear the latest sneakers, jeans, and brand-name outer garments. Some even have orange coloured and burgundy hair, 'just like Mom's' but they are also in trouble in many ways. Middle class adolescents as well as working class adolescents are using and abusing drugs and alcohol at increasing rates inside and outside of school. There are few restrictions on the sale of alcohol to minors and children, particularly at community barbecues, parties and other social gatherings. In the case of the management of child abuse, children continue to be physically and sexually abused at unacceptable rates. However, we need to understand that all the issues affecting our children emanate from common causes. If we analyze the problems of street children, abused children, children needing care and protection, or teenage pregnancies, they all have a common base. Therefore, we need to think in terms of a common approach to the solution of our children's problems. This approach must evolve from a conceptual framework that realizes the importance of spending our scarce resources on prevention programmes so that fewer of our children need the more expensive methods of intervention such as institutionalization and other specialized services. As shown in the diagram (Figure 5.1), it is more cost effective to spend our resources on the 60 percent to 80 percent of children who are at risk while they are in their own homes, than to wait until they present with more serious problems, which will require greater government expenditure over a prolonged period.

Migration of Parents

Let us also not forget that when the parent, dad or mom, migrates, children are often dumped like objects, no longer with grandmother (who is now younger and busier), but with this friend or that friend, without a second thought to the effect of long term or short term migration and separation on the child.

When the children start acting up and run away from the friends or relatives, and we begin to see a worrying increase in childhood suicides and attempted suicides in our schools, some of us shake our heads and lament on Jamaica's

Fig.5.1 Open Funnel Model. Conceptual Framework For Integrated Child Welfare Development Programme

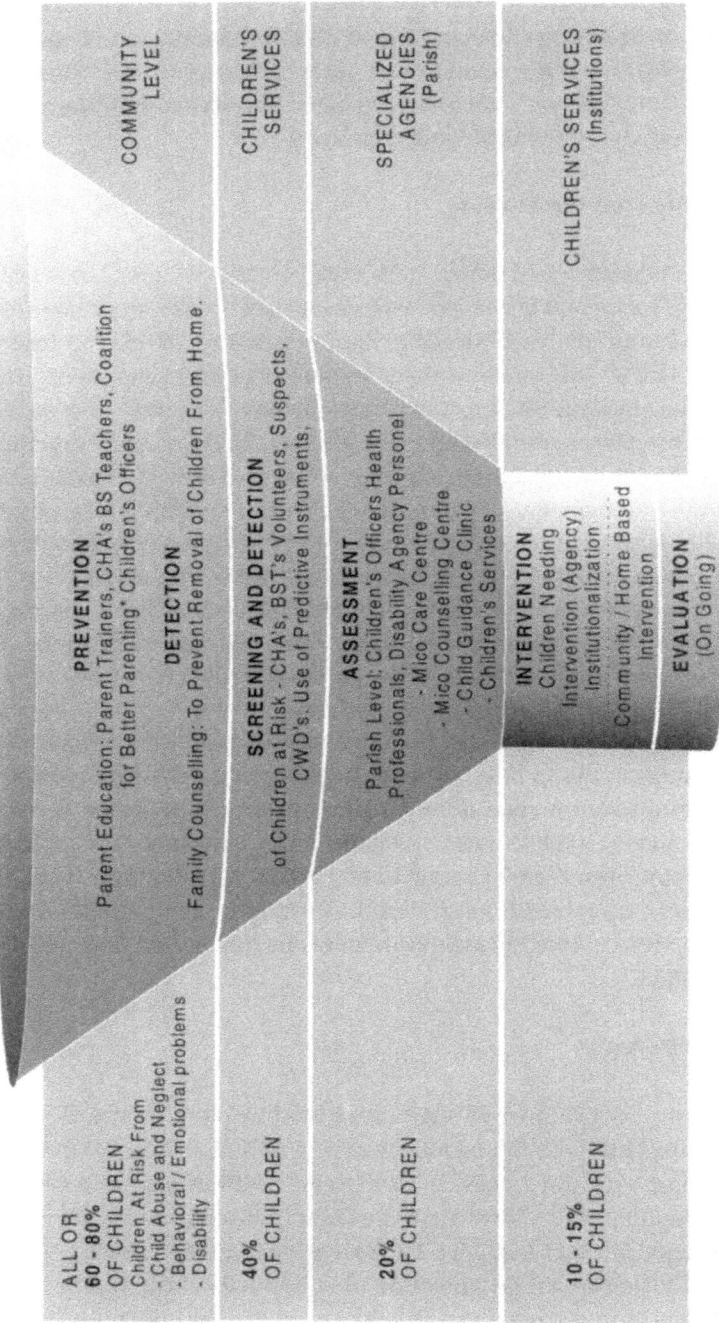

PREVENTION
Parent Education: Parent Trainers, CHA's BS Teachers, Coalition
for Better Parenting* Children's Officers

DETECTION
Family Counselling: To Prevent Removal of Children From Home.

SCREENING AND DETECTION
of Children at Risk - CHA's, BST's Volunteers, Suspects,
CWD's. Use of Predictive Instruments.

ASSESSMENT
Parish Level: Children's Officers Health
Professionals, Disability Agency Personel
- Mico Care Centre
- Mico Counselling Centre
- Child Guidance Clinic
- Children's Services

INTERVENTION
Children Needing
Intervention (Agency)
Institutionalization
Community / Home Based
Intervention

EVALUATION
(On Going)

COMMUNITY
LEVEL

CHILDREN'S
SERVICES

SPECIALIZED
AGENCIES
(Parish)

CHILDREN'S SERVICES
(Institutions)

ALL OR
60 - 80%
OF CHILDREN
Children At Risk From
- Child Abuse and Neglect
- Behavioral / Emotional problems
- Disability

40%
OF CHILDREN

20%
OF CHILDREN

10 - 15%
OF CHILDREN

Leads to: Monitoring, Review, Research, Policy Planning, Training.

This is based on the holistic approach of working with all kinds of problems - social, emotional, disability, health, etc. and all incorporates several levels of activity.
* Coalition for Better Parenting is at present mediated through the Ministry of Education Guidance and Counselling but it needs to be moved to a situation where
it can be expanded to include other cadres of trainng. *Adapted from: Working Group 'Children with Disabilities' Dec. 1995.*

future. Others of us organize Christmas treats and other activities, and we have functions and ceremonies where people give children gifts, say the right things, and appear appropriately concerned. Others of us go on talk shows on radio and on TV, and we wring our hands and agonize, but we really achieve nothing that will change the lives of these children in any meaningful way. We have to put our money where our mouths are and make a commitment to really put our children first for a prolonged period so we can pull them up out of the difficulties in which they find themselves. Let us educate our parents who have had to leave their children for economic reasons. Let us advise these parents that many of their children often lack the emotional nurturing they need and that they have to ensure that their emotional needs as well as their material needs are met. Let us support these parents and children when they need us by providing reliable guidance and counselling within and outside of the school system.

Old Time Values

We are so preoccupied with surviving economically that many of us cannot see that we are failing in our mandate to provide hope for our children's future. Journalist Betty-Ann Bowen, in 1996, wrote that many of our middle class who are fortunate to be parents had humble beginnings, yet we spoil our children by showering them with material baubles such as cellular phones and posh cars. We neglect to provide them with the important and fundamental value systems which we received as children and which they need to survive. As a society we may never be able to provide our children with three computers per class in every primary school, a free meal for every child, or fancy slides and swings for each little district and community, as obtains in the developed world, but we do not have to. They can survive and do better than those who have these things if our schools are provided with some basic equipment and supplies and if they are secure and treated as if they are special and loved.

The reality is, if we as parents pass on the correct messages about the important things in life, such as love for country and love for family, the need to respect the elderly, and respect for a supreme being (things our grandmothers taught us), we will be passing on a legacy of worth to the next generation.

Marginalization of Young Males

Another important issue is the problem that boys are not doing as well as they should be at their examinations, from Common Entrance to tertiary levels.

One educator and researcher (Miller 1994) contends that they do not have enough male teachers at the primary level and in the high and secondary school system. Other researchers cite lack of fathering as a contributing factor. We need to consciously factor some of these findings into recruitment policies in our school systems and into the curriculum of our teacher training institutions.

Family Disintegration

Many boys continue to be attracted by guns, crime and drugs, as the drug dons and criminals actively socialize them, coming into our communities and literally taking our sons away from us. Much is happening in the inner city that is causing our families to be ripped apart. Mothers have to fight to prevent dons from forming sexual alliances with their daughters, who are as young as twelve and thirteen years of age. Many parents are under tremendous pressure and feel helpless.

Support System for Families

We hear elsewhere about Mothers Against Drunk Drivers. How about mothers, fathers, parents against drugs, or parents against violence? What of husbands, or wives, or families against crime, so that parents can act as support systems for each other? These kinds of interventions are necessary to help inner city and middle income parents to cope with the demands of parenting within the context of increasing violence.

Children in the Mall

The new mall culture has been a significant feature of adolescent socialization in urban areas in the 1990s. Our middle and working class adolescents, the future leaders of our country, are now part of a new mall culture. As parents dutifully deposit them, or send them off to the malls on weekends, they are sometimes offered drugs and other illicit pleasures by teenage and adult drug pushers and prostitutes in some of our more popular shopping malls and other public places frequented by families! This is happening in one case, a few yards from one of our largest police stations. As parents, teachers, and as part of civil society, we cannot deal with this problem by simply warning our own children, or by one teacher in a single school advising her class not to go to X or Y place of business or mall. We have to tackle this problem in a much more comprehensive manner. As parents we must organize ourselves and let the owners of these commercial establishments know that they must clean up their places or we will not be patrons. We must publicly educate parents about these dangers to their children and put pressure on the business places to remove these undesirables from the family meeting places we have in our communities.

CHRISTMAS TREATS FOR CHILDREN: BALLOONS THAT BURST

Jamaican parents pride themselves on being loving, caring and committed to their children. Despite the fact that our children are being sexually abused at younger ages when compared with the developed world (Kelly 1995), and despite the fact that our children continue to be placed in police lock-ups, at Christmas time we leave no stone unturned to provide numerous treats for these same disadvantaged children, as if somehow this will compensate for 364 days of neglect. At Christmas time, service clubs, corporate bodies and other donor agencies and organizations fall over themselves in an attempt to ensure that our children, particularly those in children's homes, places of safety and our hospitals have a happy Christmas. One cannot have a problem with anyone who has the desire to engage in such activities. There is something to be said for Christmas treats, as they do help some of our most needy children to smile for a day. It does matter that a little abandoned girl can have a doll on Christmas day, or that a little four year old boy who is malnourished can eat well on New Year's Day. The point is that for the other days of the year, he has to remain in the overcrowded institution with scarce facilities, without a touch or a hug, or a kiss from someone who really cares about him. The pattern of short term, one shot approaches to the management of children's issues is symptomatic of the way in which the Jamaican society as a whole treats its children.

The Need for Sustainable Projects

For most of his existence, such a child does not have his most basic psychological need for nurturing met. He cannot then be well adjusted and whole, and able to contribute meaningfully to his society. The key point that organizations like the Children's Lobby have been communicating to the myriad agencies, service clubs and organizations that have been flooding the children's homes with money, food and gifts over the years, is that the children will eat the food in one day, and most of the little toy cars and plastic dolls will not see the light of January 2 of the next year. The resources of these organizations would therefore be better spent in sustainable projects that will benefit these children in a meaningful way in the long term. There will always be a need for some organizations to do the short term, "Christmasy" activities, but then others should be involved in funding those projects that will have an impact in the long term. For example, the staff in children's institutions are unable to provide a therapeutic environment for these children because they are not adequately trained.

1. Staff members can be sponsored for training courses in behaviour modification and other current treatment modalities that have been used successfully with emotionally damaged children in other countries that are similar to ours. One of our primary children's services agencies does not have a research officer. In one office a computer, which can provide the technology for an application system that can be used to develop a comprehensive database on children in care, their treatment plans, their reasons for being in care, etc., remains unused. Thus, many children continue to get lost in the system, no review of cases takes place, and the service agency continues to be unable to participate in the planning and policy development process for the children it serves.

2. Organizations could also assist with the funding and development of training courses in computer applications for the tracking of children and their treatment plans. Such courses can be funded at a fraction of the cost of Christmas treats and other donations made during the yuletide season. If the funds are properly managed by an independent and trustworthy body such as the Jamaica Foundation for Children (JFC), this could open up a range of opportunities for some of the nation's most disadvantaged children. This was part of the original mandate of that organization. The JFC should be encouraged to fulfill that mandate in addition to the laudable activities with which they are currently involved.

3. Interested donors could be involved in a number of other activities, such as sponsoring summer work programmes for university student(s) to develop and update appropriate and relevant databases in the main children's service agencies and their regional offices. They could help support advocacy groups (or fund the employment of short term consultants) to write operational manuals and policies in government agencies dealing with children, for example child abuse operation manuals, proper management practices for children's institutions, mandatory reporting policies for abused children.

The national policy for children should have a set framework within which programmes for children and families should take place. There are industrial policies, land policies, youth policies but a policy for children is put on the back burner for years. Having been put in place, children's service practitioners do not see it, and therefore cannot use it is a working document to improve services to the children for which it was written. We must assist the agencies with the necessary technical expertise to make the national policy for children operational.

1. We must assist these organizations to disseminate parenting and other vital information to the public on an ongoing basis. This information must be disseminated at all levels of the society and must include policy analyses, presentation and analysis of research data, and community based solutions that can be easily understood by the public. The recent changes in the media in Jamaica present challenges in this direction, for the country and the Caribbean region as a whole.
2. We must assist agencies to ensure that police officers, teachers, social workers, and doctors work as a team to solve the difficult problems, such as abandonment, child prostitution, early childhood sexual activities, which affect our children daily. We must develop a consolidated and integrated approach to service delivery to the nation's children.

There is a need for central planning in the rationalization of funds and the organizational policies for children's homes and organizations, particularly at Christmas time. This role should be assigned to an organization like the JFC in collaboration with the Child Support Unit and other policy based organizations working on behalf of children. This organization could use the technical assistance available to it through specific project teams, to advise companies on how best to use their funds, and how much to use on the short term activities (which organizations like, because it makes them look good in the press) and how much could be better spent on long term activities, which reflect a better use of their scarce resources.

Only then can we say we are truly helping this most vulnerable population. Our children need help that is meaningful. They need help that is sustainable. Our children need help that will last beyond the last balloon that bursts.

WHO WILL SAVE OUR CHILDREN?

During the past few years we have seen some of the most troubling signs of the very serious problems that children face in this country. In one week in 1996 there were seven reported deaths of children. Two children died in bus accidents, one of whom was a mere six year old boy who was the victim of callous and uncouth behaviour of adults shoving for space on a bus. Surely, the adults must share direct blame for the loss of these innocent lives. The dreadful reality of an appalling transportation system has taken on a new dimension of anarchy which is very frightening, to say the least. Many of us saw the heartrending reports on television of school children blocking a main road in St Catherine in an attempt to call attention to the extreme difficulties they face in pursuing an education. It was a terrible thing to witness the first hand reports of a number of courageous adolescent schoolgirls who complained bitterly of having to defend themselves against sexual harassment from bus conductors. The girls were determined to get an education, while the rascal conductors appeared to be as determined to treat them as pieces of meat. There have been violent shootings of teenage schoolboys in the streets of Corporate Area communities which have all the resemblances of gangland style hits. Other teenagers have been stabbed to death at school. Some have been slaughtered by gunmen while playing football and others have been killed while sleeping in their beds.

Many agencies, out of a sense of frustration, say nothing about the deaths of our children. This comes with the very disheartening realization that after children's agencies and other lobby groups make pronouncements of indignation and call on government authorities to deal directly with the underlying problems, very little, if anything at all, is ever done to make a lasting, positive impact on the situations being addressed. So the well known scenario prevails: more and more children are killed or molested; there is a chorus of shouts that such behaviour is uncivilized and unacceptable; then nothing else happens. After observing the lack of appropriate responses from the relevant agencies, one sometimes concludes that it may be futile to make either pointed, organized, sporadic or other forms of appeals on behalf of the children of this country.

A National Policy on Children and Families

Where do we go from here? The problems are large and complex, but a good place to start is in the development and enactment of a sound child and family welfare policy. It may be said that policy reflects the will of a nation to do something about its problems. If we are in fact going to give our children's services more than a facelift, the will to accomplish certain fundamental changes must be strong and well informed. The government of the day must take the responsibility to produce a comprehensive child and family policy that is implementable, accessible, workable and dynamic. Even though children are not voters – and sadly in this country, we have not had a history of a sustained and coordinated voice speaking on their behalf – this policy must now be a priority and must be made to work through the children's service agencies in a manner that can be operationalized at a practical level. Though such a policy has been written, it cannot be allowed to sit in a government agency without any relationship to the real lives of the children it was designed to serve.

Child welfare policy, like any other key policy of the society, must be planned, and based on sound empirical research and analysis. Delivery of services must be done by people who are trained to deliver top level professional services to children and their families. The days when ancillary and support staff in children's homes, for example, are chosen on the basis of being "sent" by an MP, must be put behind us, permanently. The days when a programme is adopted in Jamaica simply because someone went to "foreign" and saw it there, are long gone. Nothing is wrong in adopting tried and proven programmes or models of intervention, **but the** *ad hoc* **nature of programme implementation which has been the trade mark of child welfare policy for the past three decades must be avoided.** If we have an informed policy that can easily be made operational, at least every one will know what they are supposed to do, and who is to do what. At this point the child welfare system is not even ready for the twentieth century and it is almost time to take on the twenty first. This is mainly due to the view of succeeding governments that, because children are not voters, the budget can always be cut back in that sector in order to get the economy moving. There is the perception that every government official knows what needs to be done about children and their welfare. There is therefore little regard for empirical evidence and rational analysis in planning and policy development for child welfare and child survival programmes. As a result, succeeding governments have created a child welfare system without the coherence needed to make it work. We have to deal with our country's development in a holistic way. Our children's affairs cannot be put on hold and dealt with in a piecemeal fashion.

Collaboration Between Children's Services and Correctional Services

There is need for the Director of the Children's Services Division and the Commissioner of Corrections to collaborate in the development of a national maintenance plan, which would include an ongoing maintenance and development programme for all child care and correctional institutions. There is also need to look at the overall quality of care and service delivery in the system with a view to improving it in the long term. There is no doubt that fundamental change and additional resources and equipment are needed at all levels, and that this requires input from the level of policy making to the level of programme development. While patching here and there provides some limited relief in the short term, this narrow approach to the provision of services to children will not be enough to take us successfully into the twenty-first century.

What Needs to Be Done

Social workers, particularly those who are children's officers and correctional officers, must be involved in programme and policy development affecting their areas of service delivery. They must provide their own answers and solutions, building on what has gone before. We must involve practitioners in the planning process and challenge them to develop programmes and services to meet our unique needs and demands.

- We must have an integrated family focus in our approach to the development of policies for children, not just the disadvantaged child but for all children.
- We must incorporate preventive programmes as integral to an overall child welfare strategy, and thereby put in place a solid framework of policies and programmes which strengthen the family's ability to protect its members.
- We have to organize ourselves to do this by way of our professional associations, our NGO umbrella agencies, and service agencies, making use of the human and national resources of the universities, the Private Sector Organization of Jamaica, and the Planning Institute of Jamaica, as well as the international donor community.

If we fail to grasp this moment, and fail to do something constructive and sustainable, we will have failed our children, as a society, as parents, and as representatives of our generation.

The Role of the Child Support Unit and the Planning Institute of Jamaica

We need rational planning and sustainable systems, not only for the industrial and business sectors, but for the social sector as well. We need efficient management, especially in the sectors of our society that cater to children, particularly those in difficult circumstances. Our Children's Services Division should be the most efficient and effective department of government as it has an important role to play in controlling deviance. For too long, policy makers and leaders have paid lip service to our nation's children and have allowed services for children to become the "Cinderella" of the government service.

There are special problems facing the younger members of our society as our society changes, and yet we do not see the social services sector evolving and developing in the way that we see the industrial and economic sectors changing. If we take a look at the press coverage of the plight of children in institutions over the years, we see that the two major problems related to child care are substandard physical facilities and inadequate support services. In addition there are other, more serious problems facing these children, which never come to public attention. Inasmuch as we all have some responsibility to take care of the needs of children, special responsibilities fall to those who formulate and implement policy. The Child Support Unit and the Planning Institute of Jamaica have special responsibilities for policy development for children. Few policies have been enacted by successive governments that have made a fundamental difference to the quality and degree of the human or material resources that are put into the child welfare sector in particular. As the degree of violence increases in our society towards the end of the decade, few of us realize that we are reaping the seeds of our prolonged neglect of effective policy development for our nation's children. It is recommended that PIOJ, through the Child Support Unit, should seek to focus on one or two burning issues affecting children per year, working on a project basis, with a view to dealing with the root causes. As shown in Figure 5.2, each project could be monitored by an advisory group or committee. The mandate of such a committee would be to harness the necessary technical resources not only to treat the children experiencing the problem, but also to decrease the incidence of the problem in the society within a specific time period. The role of the advocacy and policy development committee (shown in the diagram) would be to coordinate these two important tasks for the other projects.

Another policy issue that needs to be addressed by the PIOJ is the development of a strong prevention component to the child welfare policy. The child welfare system, as well as the education system, must also address the issue of early detection and treatment of emotional and behavioural problems of our children as a major prevention policy initiative, to reduce the trauma to both the child and the society at large in later years. Children with emotional and behavioural problems produce offspring who will, in turn, present with similar problems or worse in the next generation. Many such problems are treatable when detected early. This is one issue where neglect will most certainly lead to a situation where the penal system will be struggling to deal with the consequences at a later date. This effort will require careful collaboration between all parties concerned and will need assistance from

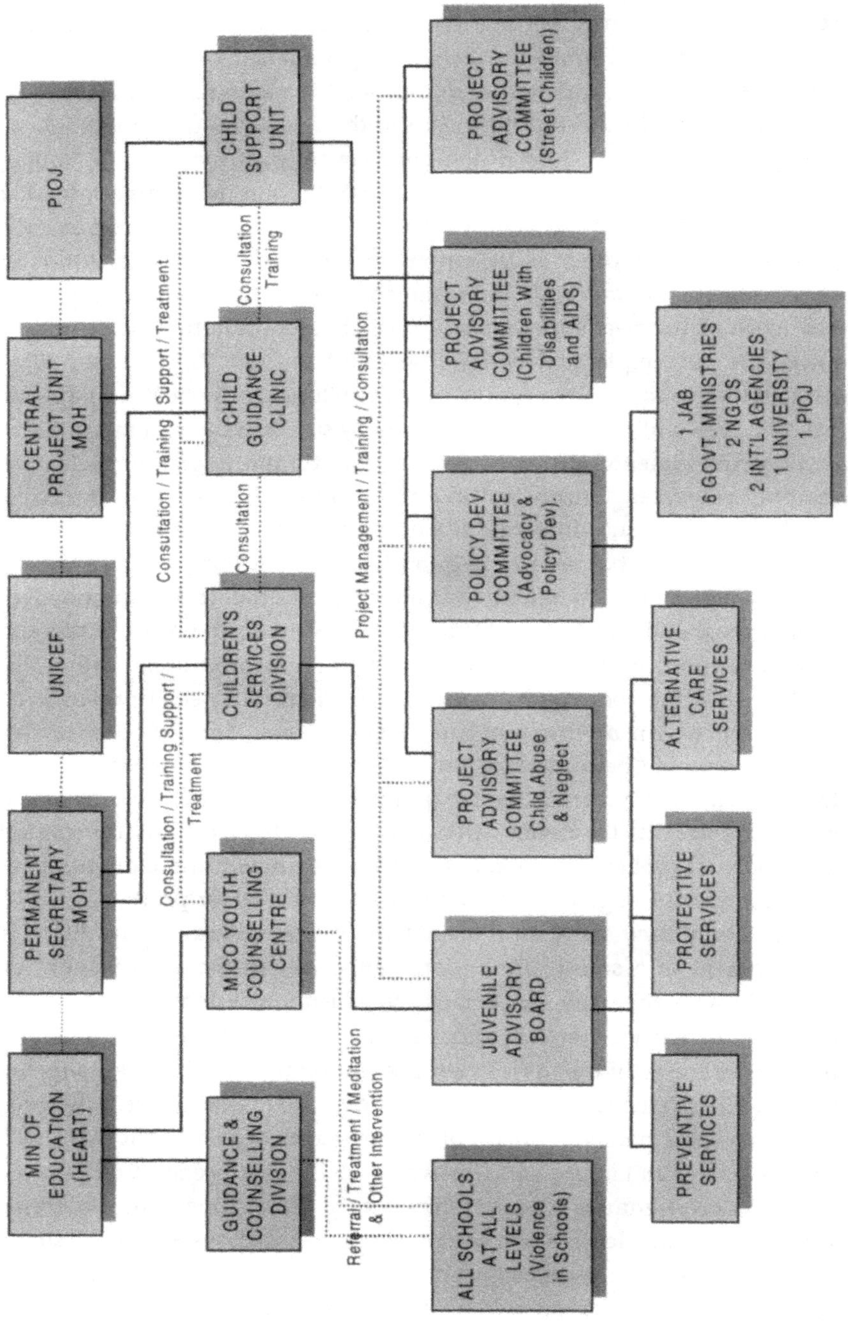

Fig.5.2 *Role of Coordinating Bodies in an Integrated System of Project Management*

social service agencies, researchers in and out of academia, as well as professional bodies such as the Pediatric Association of Jamaica, The Jamaica Teachers Association and The Jamaica Association of Social Workers. When a structured approach is taken, and issues related to child care are pursued with ongoing diligence, then the society may be able to look forward to Child Month each year as a time to celebrate our gains, to re-evaluate our direction and focus, to inform and educate the public regarding child care issues and to re-galvanise our sense of purpose to strive for more and more real gains in this important area of nation building.

The area of children in institutions is one which can benefit from a national policy on children and families. Such a policy can help us to decide if we should be building more of the same type of child care institutions and whether we should continue to manage them in the way they are presently operated. Should we not be providing and operating facilities that will focus more on therapeutic work rather than simply custodial services in attempting to help children in difficult circumstances? Or should we be focused on other alternatives completely, such as adequate foster care and adoption? Should we create (not necessarily build) institutions that specialize in large scale behaviour modification while others specialize in skills training and life skills development, for example? These issues need to be clarified and decided.

The other major problem is the lack of trained clinical staff to do the intensive clinical work that is necessary to deal with the serious emotional and psychological problems of children in institutions. We hear children speaking of deep seated feelings of rejection and being abandoned, of attacking and hurting their parents, of feelings of worthlessness and low self esteem. These are common causes of maladjustment, promiscuity, aggression, violent and suicidal behaviour and the children are crying out to their parents for attention. Administrators speak to the need for clinical intervention with these children year after year to no avail. In reality, though the University of the West Indies has been training professionals to do this type of work for 30 years, many of these professionals do not return to work in the system; therefore, the child welfare system remains ill-equipped to deal with the emotional and psychological needs of these children in a comprehensive manner.

WE ARE PEOPLE TOO

The following speech was written and presented by two ten year olds at a Children's Lobby Awards function for Child Advocates held at the Senior Common Room, University of the West Indies in May 1994. It was printed in the Children's Advocate *as a report from the Jamaica Coalition on the Rights of the Child in October 1996, and is reproduced here with the authors' permission.*

l-r *Selena Cowan and Janelle Brown speaking at the Child Advocates Award Function.*

We would like to welcome you to this inaugural Child Advocates Awards luncheon. To begin this afternoon's deliberations, my friend and I would like to make a statement on behalf of the children of Jamaica.

We the children of Jamaica are crying out for attention, whether we are rich or poor; sick or healthy; black, brown, white or yellow. Many of us are neglected, abandoned, abused, and in some cases, murdered. We are appealing to you who are here today, social workers, lawyers, doctors and other people in positions of authority in our country, to do something that will have a positive impact on these problems that we are facing.

One of the ways that we think adults can help us as children is to listen to what we have to say. Please hear us out. We are people too, and we sometimes think of things that haven't even crossed your minds. We also have good ideas that adults and children alike may benefit from. For example, when parents are divorced, parents sometimes use their children as weapons against each other. If they just stop to think that the children are being torn apart by this and may be left with emotional scars which may last for the rest of their lives, they would not do this to their children.

We keep hearing that we are the leaders of the future and the people of tomorrow. Should the future leaders of Jamaica be left on the streets to fend for themselves? We think not. Should the people of tomorrow be allowed to become prostitutes at the age of eight? We think not. Should the future leaders, parents, and the members of our society, be physically, emotionally or sexually abused by individuals who are supposed to be responsible adults? We think not. Should children, the nation's future, be bullied, verbally attacked, pushed off buses, simply because we are children? We think not! Ladies and gentlemen, we are asking you to do something about our problems. We love and respect you; we are asking you to love and respect us in return.

We thank you for hearing our voices today, on behalf of all the children of Jamaica. Please help us!

May 15, 1994

NOTE

1. Source of 1996 data: Police Statistical Unit, Kingston, Jamaica.

RESOURCE MATERIAL

Books and Documents

David and Lucille Packard Foundation. 1992. *The Future of Children*. School-Linked Services, Vol. 2, No. 1, Los Angeles, California: Centre for the Future of Children.

Harvard Educational Review. 1974. *The Rights of Children*.

Jamaica Coalition on the Rights of the Child. 1996. *Children Have Rights Too*. Kingston, Jamaica: UNICEF.

Jamaica Foundation for Children. 1994. *Children: Today's Children, Tomorrow's World*. Kingston, Jamaica: UNICEF.

Levy, H., Chevannes, B. 1996. *They Cry Respect: Urban Violence and Poverty in Jamaica*. Kingston, Jamaica: Centre for Population, Community and Social Change, Department of Sociology and Social Work, University of the West Indies.

Planning Institute of Jamaica. *The National Plan of Action: Goals for Jamaican Children to the Year 2000*. Kingston, Jamaica: UNICEF.

Stelle, M., Margna, M. 1994. *Strengthening Multi-Ethnic Families and Communities, A Violence Prevention Training Programme*, Los Angeles, California: Consulting and Clinical Services.

Referral Sources and Agency Contacts

(a) **Advocacy, Policy Development, Research Dissemination**

The Children's Lobby
3a Manhattan Road
Kingston 5

The Jamaica Foundation for Children
1A Hope Road
Kingston 7

The Jamaica Coalition
on the Rights of the Child
Swallowfield Road
Kingston 5

United Nations Children's
Fund (UNICEF)
Knutsford Boulevard
Kingston 5

Child Month Committee
c/o The Children's Services Division
10a Chelsea Avenue
Kingston 5

Children First
c/o YMCA (Young Men's
Christian Association)
19 Monk Street
Spanish Town

CVSS (Council of Voluntary
Social Services)
122-126 Tower Street
Kingston

Western Alliance for the
Upliftment of Children Project
c/o British Save the Children Fund
1 National Heroes Circle
Kingston

(b) **Agencies Offering Recreational and Training Services to Children and Youth**

Youth to Youth
c/o Priory High School
32 Hope Road
Kingston 10

The Girl Guides Association of Jamaica
2 Waterloo Road
Kingston 10

Girls Town Jamaica
89 Maxfield Avenue
Kingston 13

The Boys Scouts Association
Camp Road
Kingston 5
The Girls Brigade
2e Camp Road
Kingston 5

The Boys Brigade
2e Camp Road
Kingston 5

STEP (Skills, Training and
Empowerment Programme)
c/o Social Development Commission
22 Camp Road
Kingston 4

HEART (Human Employment
and Resource Training)
4 Park Boulevard
Kingston 5

Boys Town Industrial Training Centre
6 Collie Smith Drive
Kingston 12

Bibliography

Barland, M., ed. 1976. *Violence in the Family*. Atlantic Highlands, NJ: Humanities Press.

Betse, H., Richardson, .1981.*Developing Life Story Book Programmes for Foster Children*. Child Welfare, Vol. LX, No. 8. New York: Child Welfare League of America.

Bowlby, J. 1953. *Child Care and the Growth of Love*. London: Pelican Books.

Brodber, E. 1972. *Abandonment of Children in Jamaica*. Kingston, Jamaica: Institute of Social and Economic Research, University of the West Indies.

Child Guidance Clinic. 1995.

Cooper, D. 1976. *The Death of the Family*. New York: Penguin Books.

Coser, R., ed. 1974. *The Family: Its Structures and Functions*. Stony Brook, NY: State University of New York, Family Service Association of America.

Crawford-Brown, C. 1986. *Survey of Services for Children in Jamaica, Survey of Services for Children in the Caribbean*. Kingston, Jamaica: Caribbean Child Development Centre, University of the West Indies.

———. 1987. *An Analysis of the Jamaican Child Welfare System*, Occasional Paper Series, No. 1. Kingston, Jamaica: Department of Sociology and Social Work, University of the West Indies.

———. 1993. Factors Associated with Conduct Disorder in Jamaican Male Adolescents. Doctoral dissertation. New Brunswick, NJ: Rutgers University.

Crawford-Brown, C., Rattray, M. 1994. The Barrel Children of Jamaica: The Sociocultural Context of Caribbean Migration. Unpublished study. Kingston, Jamaica: Department of Sociology and Social Work, University of the West Indies.

David, G. 1967. *Patterns of Social Functioning in Family Relationships: Natural and Parent-Child Problems*. Toronto: University of Toronto School of Social Work.

Economic and Social Survey Jamaica 1992.

Ennew, J. 1986. *Street and Working Children, A Guide to Planning*. Development Manual 4. London: Save the Children U.K.

Felker, E. 1975. *Foster-Parenting Young Children: Guidelines From a Foster Parent*. New York: Child Welfare League of America.

Fox Harding, L. 1996. *The Family, the State and Social Policy*. London: MacMillan Press.

Friel, L. 1973. *Components of a System of Child Welfare.* Boston, Massachusetts: Committee on Children and Youth.

Frosh, S., Glaser, D. 1988. *Child Sexual Abuse.* London: MacMillan Education.

Girvan, N., ed. 1997. *Poverty, Empowerment and Social Development in the Caribbean.* Kingston, Jamaica: Canoe Press.

Glazer, N., Creedon, C. 1970. *Children and Poverty: Some Sociological and Psychological Perspectives.* Chicago: Rand McNally.

Hess, P., Howard, T. 1981. *An Ecological Model for Assessing Psychological Difficulties in Children,* Child Welfare Vol. LX, No. 8. New York: Child Welfare League of America.

Jones, E. 1986. "The social status of the Jamaican child". Paper presented at the First Children's Lobby Conference of Child Advocates, Caenwood Centre, Ministry of Education, Youth and Culture.

Kadushin, A. 1967. *Child Welfare Services.* New York: Macmillan.

Kelly, L. 1995. *Surviving Sexual Violence.* London: Polity Press.

Levy, H., Chevannes, B. 1996. *They Cry Respect: Urban Violence and Poverty in Jamaica.* Kingston, Jamaica: Centre for Population, Community and Social Change, Department of Sociology and Social Work, University of the West Indies.

Marsh, O.D. 1994. *Children in Especially Difficult Circumstances, Policy Development and Review of Legislation in Jamaica.* Kingston, Jamaica: Child Support Unit, Ministry of Youth and Local Government, UNICEF.

Mass, H.S., Engler, E. 1959. *Children in Need of Parents.* New York: Columbia University Press.

Milbourne, P. 1995. *Child Abuse in Jamaica.* Kingston, Jamaica: UNICEF.

Morrison, L. 1995. *Teach me a Better Way to Live.* Kingston, Jamaica: G&M Associates.

Patterson, V., Wood, K. 1993. Unpublished study of child care institutions in Kingston and St Andrew. Kingston, Jamaica: Department of Sociology and Social Work, University of the West Indies.

Planning Institute of Jamaica (PIOJ). 1992. *Situation Analysis of Women and Children in Jamaica.* Kingston, Jamaica: PIOJ.

———. 1995a. *Survey of Living Conditions.* Kingston, Jamaica: PIOJ.

———. 1995b. *The National Plan of Action: Goals for Jamaican Children to the Year 2000.* Kingston, Jamaica: UNICEF.

———. 1995c. *Situation Analysis of Women and Children in Jamaica.* Kingston, Jamaica: UNICEF.

Reiner, B., Kaufman, I. 1963. *Character Disorders in Parents of Delinquents.* New York: Family Services Association of America.

Ritter, B. 1988. *Sometimes God Has a Kid's Face: The Story of America's Exploited Street Children.* New York: Covenant House.

Rosse, A.S., Kegan, J., Hareven, T., eds. 1978. *The Family.* New York: W.W. Norton.

Sabatini, F., Newman-Williams, S. 1997. *Child Poverty in the Caribbean.* In Girvan, N., ed. *Poverty, Empowerment and Social Development in the Caribbean.* Kingston, Jamaica: Canoe Press.

Sayle, E. 1994. *The First Fifty Years.* Kingston, Jamaica: Kingston Publishers.

Semaj, L., Redfearn, C. 1986. An Evaluation of Children's Homes in Jamaica. Unpublished study. Kingston, Jamaica: Caribbean Child Development Centre.

Thomas-Hope, E. 1992. *Explanation in Caribbean Migration*. Warwick University Caribbean Studies. London: MacMillan Press.

Tomlinson, R., Petos, P. 1981. "Alternatives to placing children: therapy with disengaged families", *Child Welfare: Journal of Policy, Practice and Programme* 60 No. 2.

United Nations Children's Fund (UNICEF). 1986. *Children at Risk in Jamaica Data Sheet*. Kingston, Jamaica: UNICEF.

Warsh, R., Maluccio, A., Pine, B. 1994. *Teaching Family Reunification: A Source Book*. Washington, DC: The Child Welfare League.

Wilson, L., Green, J. 1983. "An experiential approach to cultural awareness in child welfare", *Child Welfare: Journal of Policy, Practice and Programme* 62 No. 4.

Index

www.ingramcontent.com/pod-product-compliance
Lightning Source LLC
Chambersburg PA
CBHW030653270326
41929CB00007B/347